BROWNS
ESSENTIAL

Everything You Need to Know to Be a Real Fan!

Mary Schmitt Boyer

TRIUMPH
BOOKS

CHICAGO

Library of Congress Cataloging-in-Publication Data

Boyer, Mary Schmitt.
    Browns essential : everything you need to know to be a real fan! /
Mary Schmitt Boyer.
      p. cm.
    Includes bibliographical references.
    ISBN-13: 978-1-57243-873-6 (hard cover)
    ISBN-10: 1-57243-873-8 (hard cover)
      1. Cleveland Browns (Football team : 1946–1995)—History. 2.
    Cleveland Browns (Football team : 1999–)—History. I. Title.

GV956.C6B69 2006
796.332'640977132—dc22

                                                    2006003207

This book is available in quantity at special discounts for your group or organization. For further information, contact:

Triumph Books
542 South Dearborn Street
Suite 750
Chicago, Illinois 60605
(312) 939-3330
Fax (312) 663-3557

Printed in U.S.A.
ISBN-13: 978-1-57243-873-6
ISBN-10: 1-57243-873-8
Design by Patricia Frey
All photos courtesy of AP/Wide World Photos except where otherwise indicated

For Daddy.

He'd love this, even though he wasn't a huge football fan. I have to admit I could never adequately answer his most pressing question about the game: "Why does the guy with the ball always run into all those other guys?"

And for Gene.

Just because.

Contents

Foreword

Tradition is an important concept in the world of sports, and it's a key component of the rich history of the Cleveland Browns. That tradition started when Otto Graham, Marion Motley, Lou Groza, and company formed a dynasty under Paul Brown in the late 1940s and early 1950s. It carried on to include 15 Hall of Famers, the greatest running back of all time, the underdog 1964 world championship team, the overachieving Kardiac Kids, a hit record titled "Bernie, Bernie," and painful words like "Red Right 88," "The Drive," "The Fumble," and "The Move."

I always thought another part of the tradition was the generations of loyal fans bringing their children to games on the lakefront, and those kids growing up and bringing their children to "The House of Thrills"— as my good friend Casey Coleman calls it.

In *Browns Essential*, Mary Schmitt Boyer has put together a book that covers all aspects of the tradition of the Browns. Having been involved with the Browns as a player and broadcaster since 1971, I've heard many stories about the good old days and lived through some pretty good times myself. *Browns Essential* refreshed my memory on lots of those and even exposed me to some new information about the team.

This book will do the same for you. You'll find out how the team got started, what made it so successful, and even who I selected as my all-time toughest Brown. After learning about the coaches, the players, and the games, you can put your new knowledge to the test with the pop quizzes scattered throughout the book. The answers might even win you a cocktail or two in a game of Browns football trivia.

Boyer not only captures the tradition and history of the team, she even takes you behind the scenes and introduces you to the players' choice for MVP for many years, Dino Lucarelli. People have heard of many players since the Browns started in 1946, but Lucarelli might be the only man to have met just about every one of them. He's the ultimate "unsung hero" of the Browns, and Boyer gives him his long-overdue recognition.

In reading Boyer's book I often found myself saying, "I forgot about that," and I'm sure you will, too. In fact, every once in a while you might even say, "I didn't know that." I know I did.

So button your chin strap, smear on some eye black, tape your ankles, and put on your Dawg mask (if you must) for this trip down memory lane. Revisit the tradition, and, most of all, keep the faith.

—Doug Dieken

Acknowledgments

Any project of this type requires a great deal of help from a great number of sources. It could not have been completed without the assistance of Browns Manager of Alumni Relations Dino Lucarelli, Ravens Senior Vice President of Public and Community Relations Kevin Byrne, Browns Vice President of Communications Bill Bonsiewicz, Ken Mather and Amy Palcic of the Browns publicity/media relations department, Cincinnati Bengals Public Relations Director Jack Brennan, and Massillon Washington Athletics Director Jeff Thornberry. Thanks to all of them for helping to set up interviews, and thanks to those who agreed to be interviewed.

I am indebted to all the *Plain Dealer* writers who have covered the Browns so thoroughly over the years, especially colleagues Bob Dolgan (for his flair in writing historical pieces and obituaries) and Bill Livingston and Dennis Manoloff (for their insights). Thanks, too, to Patti Graziano and her staff in the *Plain Dealer* news research department and to the writers from the *Akron Beacon Journal*.

While researching the history of the Browns, I read all or parts of the following books:

Tales from the Browns Sideline by Tony Grossi, *When All the World Was Browns Town* by Terry Pluto, *PB: The Paul Brown Story* by Paul Brown with Jack Clary, *Cleveland Browns A to Z* and *Cleveland Browns Facts and Trivia* by Roger Gordon, *Legends by the Lake* by John Keim, *The Cleveland Browns: The Great Tradition* edited by Bob Moon, *Brown's Town* by Alan Natali, *Out of Bounds* by Jim Brown with Steve Delshon, *Fumble! The Browns, Modell and the Move* by Michael G. Poplar with James A. Toman, *Browns Memories* by Tim Long, *On Being Brown* by

Scott Huler, *Pressure* by Sam Rutigliano, *The Education of a Coach* by David Halberstam, and *Cleveland Stadium: The Last Chapter* by James A. Toman and Gregory G. Deegan. My thanks to the authors and editors for their insights.

The Birth of the Browns

Arthur B. "Mickey" McBride was an unlikely football team owner. A paperboy who grew up to become a newspaper executive in Chicago and Cleveland, he also owned real estate in addition to a cab company, a radio station, a printing company, and a horse racing wire syndicate.

He never had much use for football until one fall when he went to visit his son, Arthur Jr., at the University of Notre Dame, where he attended a game and fell in love with the sport. He came home and started to follow the struggling Cleveland Rams of the National Football League, a team having a tough time trying to stay afloat. Five losing seasons after its inception in 1937, owner Homer Marshman sold the team to Daniel F. Reeves and Fred Levy Jr. in 1941, although Reeves bought out Levy a couple years later. The team suspended operations in 1943, and rumors flew that they were preparing to leave town. Yet Reeves rejected McBride's offer to purchase the team.

McBride was undaunted. He had heard about a new league—the All-America Football Conference (AAFC)—that was being formed by Arch Ward, the sports editor of the *Chicago Tribune*. Ward was more than happy to have McBride's enthusiasm—and his money—join the league, so he granted Cleveland a franchise in 1944. The league planned to open play in 1946 with Cleveland and seven other teams—the Brooklyn Dodgers, the Buffalo Bisons, the Chicago Rockets, the Los Angeles Dons, the Miami Seahawks (who would move to Baltimore and become the Colts after the league's first season), the New York Yankees, and the San Francisco 49ers.

After McBride secured his franchise (with the help of Cleveland businessman Robert H. Gries), he hired Paul Brown as coach and then decided to hold a newspaper contest to name the team. The winner was

1

Starting Lineup

Starting Lineup for the Original Cleveland Browns (1946)

Offense

LE	No. 58	Mac Speedie
LT	No. 40	Jim Daniell
	No. 48	Ernie Blandin
LG	No. 36	Ed Ulinski
C	No. 20	Mike Scarry
RG	No. 32	Lin Houston
	No. 30	Bill Willis
RT	No. 44	Lou Rymkus
RE	No. 56	Dante Lavelli
	No. 50	John Yonakor
QB	No. 60	Otto Graham
RB	No. 90	Edgar Jones
	No. 85	Don Greenwood
FB	No. 76	Marion Motley

Defense

LE	No. 52	George Young
	No. 55	John Harrington
LT	No. 48	Ernie Blandin
	No. 40	Jim Daniell
MG	No. 30	Bill Willis
RT	No. 42	Chet Adams
	No. 49	Len Simonetti
RE	No. 50	John Yonakor
LLB	No. 76	Marion Motley
MLB	No. 66	Lou Saban
RLB	No. 20	Mike Scarry
LCB	No. 85	Don Greenwood
	No. 82	Bill Lund
RCB	No. 92	Tom Colella
S	No. 62	Cliff Lewis

promised a $1,000 war bond. There were many entries suggesting the team be called the Browns in honor of the much-respected coach, but Brown wasn't comfortable with that notion. So the team became the Panthers, earning John J. Harnett, a young sailor, the war bond.

Not long after that, George Jones, former owner of a semipro team from the 1920s also called the Cleveland Panthers, approached McBride. Jones felt he still owned the rights to the name, and he wanted McBride to pay for them. McBride declined, partly because he and Coach Brown didn't want to have any connection to a franchise that had failed. At that point the coach finally agreed to let the team be named the Browns.

The team's colors were to be brown (obviously) and orange, which happened to match the colors of the site of the team's first training camp—Bowling Green State University. The Browns uniforms were unadorned, a tradition that continues to this day.

It didn't take the team long to establish itself. They won their first exhibition game, beating the Brooklyn Dodgers 35–20 on August 30, 1946, before a crowd of 35,964 in Akron's Rubber Bowl. In their regular-season debut, on September 6, 1946, they crushed the Miami Seahawks 44–0 before a crowd of 60,135. That crowd was almost twice as big as the 32,178 that watched the Cleveland Rams win the 1945 NFL championship 15–14 over the Washington Redskins and star quarterback Sammy Baugh. Discouraged by the lack of support, the Rams pulled up stakes and moved to Los Angeles, leaving the Browns as the only (football) team in town.

But what a team they were! From that first exhibition game through the four-year existence of the AAFC, the Browns dominated the league. In fact, they rolled through those four seasons with a 52–4–3 record and won four titles. They were the only champions the AAFC ever had.

Brown put together a strong team of talented players. Some of them had played for the Rams and elected to stay in Cleveland when that team left town. Others, like Dante Lavelli and Marion Motley, had played for Coach Brown before. Quarterback Otto Graham, a

TRIVIA

Who started at quarterback for the Browns in their first AAFC game?

Answers to the trivia questions are on pages 159–160.

3

The 1947 Browns offense strikes a pose at Cleveland Municipal Stadium. Photo
courtesy of Bettmann/CORBIS.

newcomer and a Northwestern alumnus, proved to be the perfect fit for the
franchise for years to come.

A victory over the Miami Seahawks was the start of a seven-game
winning streak for the new Browns. In addition to shutting out Miami,
the Browns blanked Buffalo 28–0 and the New York Yankees 7–0. The
Browns lost back-to-back games to the San Francisco 49ers and the Los
Angeles Dons in the middle of the season, but they finished the season
with a five-game winning streak, including a 66–14 victory at Brooklyn
on December 8.

The Browns won the Western Division title with a 12–2 record and
were to face the Yankees for the first AAFC title on December 22, 1946. But
there was controversy heading into the game. Captain and starting tackle
Jim Daniell was involved in a scuffle with Cleveland police and was
arrested for public intoxication. Fellow offensive linemen Mac Speedie

and Lou Rymkus were charged with disorderly conduct in the incident. Coach Brown cut Daniell for violating a team rule prohibiting drinking during the season.

Even without Daniell, the Browns beat the Yankees 14–9, scoring the winning touchdown on a 16-yard pass from Graham to Lavelli late in the game.

Incidentally, Daniell was later cleared of the charge of public intoxication, but Coach Brown did not ask him back. In fact, although Brown traded Daniell's rights to the Chicago Rockets, Daniell never played professional football again.

The Browns' second season went much as their first. The defending champions opened with a 30–14 victory over Buffalo, starting a five-game winning streak. They finished the season 12–1–1 and again beat the Yankees, 14–3, for their second straight championship. The league selected Graham as its most valuable player, and Brown was named coach of the year by *Pro Football Illustrated*.

Those two seasons served only as a warm-up for the third season, in which the Browns put together a perfect 14–0 record, becoming one of only three pro football teams ever to go undefeated. (The 1937 Los Angeles Bulldogs went 8–0 in the American Football League, and the 1972 Miami Dolphins went 17–0 in the National Football League.) The Browns beat Buffalo 49–7 in the championship game on December 19, 1948. They outscored their opponents 389–190 that season. Graham shared the league's Most Valuable Player award with San Francisco quarterback Frankie Albert, and Brown was named Coach of the Year by the *New York Daily News*.

In 1949 the Browns continued their excellence on the field, but the league was struggling. Brooklyn and New York merged for the 1949 season, bringing the league down to seven teams. The fact of the matter was that the Browns had become so predictably successful (San Francisco and Los Angeles were the only teams to beat them in the four-year history of the AAFC) that attendance started dropping off. High player salaries and travel costs combined with low attendance did not make for financial success. After the Browns waltzed through the regular season with a 9–1–2 record—beating Buffalo 31–21 in the playoffs and then triumphing over San Francisco 21–7 in the title game—the league collapsed.

McBride, who may have been the only owner making money, did all he could to try to remedy the situation, even offering to bail out the other franchises. But in the end he was fighting a losing battle. Just before the Browns won their fourth and final AAFC crown, the National Football League announced that Cleveland, San Francisco, and Baltimore would join the NFL for the 1950 season. Players from the remaining teams would be made available in a dispersal draft.

Whether the Browns' final victory over San Francisco was emblematic of what was to come for the team or just anticlimactic is open to debate. But there is no question that the Browns were the class act of the AAFC, a distinction they carried with them into the NFL.

Paul Brown: A Remarkable Life in Football

It sounds ridiculous—if not sacrilegious—to say it now, but Paul Brown was not Browns owner Mickey McBride's first choice to coach the team. Given that McBride fell in love with the game while watching a contest at the University of Notre Dame while visiting his son, Arthur Jr., it should come as no surprise that he first sought to hire Fighting Irish coach Frank Leahy.

Leahy had compiled an impressive 32–5–3 record in his first four seasons at the helm for Notre Dame, including a national championship in 1943. Naturally, the university was loath to part with him, so McBride was forced to turn his attention elsewhere. It may have been the best thing that could have happened to the Browns. After all, what kind of team nickname would "the Leahys" have been?

In an unusual development that certainly would not happen today, McBride sought the advice of newspapermen to help him select a coach. First he turned to John Dietrich, football writer for *The Plain Dealer*, who urged McBride to hire Brown, a native of Norwalk, Ohio, who had attended Washington High School in Massillon and transferred from Ohio State to that cradle of coaches, Miami University.

Brown already was well on his way to legendary status at that time. He was only 21 years old when he was named coach at Severn Prep, which was run by the navy. In two years his teams achieved a 16–1–1 record, more than good enough to qualify him as head coach for his high school alma mater. In nine seasons at Washington High, Brown's teams went 80–8–2, winning six state titles and four national championships. The fans were so enamored with their coach that they built a 21,000-seat stadium and named it after him. To this day it is used as the sight for some of the Ohio state high school football championships.

A wave of public support swept Brown in as the replacement for Francis Schmidt at Ohio State, a position Brown called his "ultimate dream." From 1941 to 1943 the Buckeyes went 18–8–1, winning the national championship in 1942. Even a stint in the navy didn't interrupt Brown's success—he led the Great Lakes Naval Training Center to a 15–5–2 record in two seasons.

Despite Brown's stellar record, McBride still wanted additional confirmation; he got it from Arch Ward, sports editor of the *Chicago Tribune* and founder of the league McBride was set to join. Ward even helped recruit Brown, and the 36-year-old coach actually signed his first contract—for five years and $125,000—in Ward's office on February 9, 1945.

That contract established a system—a way of doing things—that the Browns would follow for years to come. Brown, using Major League

Paul Brown was a no-nonsense coach. Photo courtesy of Diamond Images.

DID YOU KNOW . . . That Paul Brown was voted College Coach of the Year in 1942 after Ohio State won the national title? However, he agreed to forgo the award so it could be presented instead to Georgia Tech coach Bill Alexander, who was dying.

Baseball's New York Yankees as a role model, had rules—lots of them. Following them was mandatory—breaking them was not an option for any player who hoped to remain with the team. Starting left tackle Jim Daniell found that out the hard way. Arrested and charged with public intoxication—a charge he was cleared of later—Daniell was cut by Brown the week before the first AAFC Championship game in 1946.

In his 1997 book, *"When All the World Was Browns Town,"* Akron *Beacon Journal* columnist Terry Pluto detailed some of Brown's rules. Players could not smoke, drink, or swear around him. They had to wear sport coats and ties in public. Dirty T-shirts were forbidden at practice, and dress shirts were required for dinner. He refused to let players drink water during practice because he thought it caused cramps. He instituted a 10:00 PM curfew the night before games and became the first coach to have his players stay in a hotel the night before *home* games as well as road games. And oh, yes, he also asked his players to refrain from having sex from Tuesday night until after the game.

According to Pluto, players said Brown's idea of the perfect pregame meal was a steak with no ketchup, a salad with no dressing, and a baked potato with no butter or sour cream.

Steely eyed and intense, Brown never swore and never raised his voice. He didn't need to—he could cut a player to the quick with a well-chosen word or comment. Yet football was not his entire life. He and his staff were usually done for the day in time for Brown to enjoy dinner with his wife, Katy, and their three sons.

Brown's genius and influence would eventually be felt far beyond Cleveland. Some of the practices he established would become commonplace throughout the league. For instance when star quarterback Otto Graham needed 15 stitches to close a gash after he was elbowed in the mouth by San Francisco 49er Art Michalik in 1953, Brown fashioned a plastic bar to be placed across the front of Graham's helmet to protect the injury—a precursor to today's face masks.

TOP SIX

Most Memorable Games (According to Paul Brown in his autobiography PB: The Paul Brown Story)

1. His first victory over Canton-McKinley High School, 6–0, in 1935 (his fourth season at Washington High)
2. Ohio State's 20–20 tie versus Michigan in 1941
3. Great Lakes Naval Training Center's 39–7 victory over Notre Dame in 1945
4. Cleveland's 35–10 victory over the defending NFL champion Philadelphia Eagles in the Browns' NFL debut in 1950
5. Cleveland's 30–28 victory over the Los Angeles Rams (formerly of Cleveland) for the 1950 NFL championship
6. Cincinnati's 14–10 victory over Cleveland at Cincinnati in 1970, the second regular-season meeting between the two teams (Cleveland won the first meeting at home)

Brown was the first coach to hire a full-time staff and a full-time scouting department. He was the first coach to provide his players with playbooks—and the first to give tests on those playbooks. In fact, he was the first coach to test the intelligence of his players before drafting them and the first to time them in the 40-yard dash. He was the first coach to analyze film clips and grade his players based on analyses of those clips. He was the first coach to call plays from the sideline and to use substitutions to deliver those plays to his quarterback. He was the inventor of the draw play, the flea flicker pass, and a style of play featuring short passes that would later became known as the ubiquitous West Coast offense.

Brown also created the "taxi squad," a concept that allowed several nonroster players to practice with the team and be available in case of injury. The players were not on the team's payroll, however. They were paid directly by McBride, who also happened to own a cab company, which was the source of the nickname.

Another common football term that can be traced back to Brown is *blitz*, a word used to describe a play in which the linebackers and/or defensive backs rush the quarterback. The term is derived from the German word *blitzkrieg*, an all-out air and land offensive.

Though Brown's time in Cleveland was glorious at the start—the team played for a championship in each of its first 10 seasons and won seven—it ended badly. In spite of a 167–53–8 record, a .725 winning percentage, and just one losing season in 17 years, Brown was fired by Art Modell in 1963.

Four years later Brown was enshrined in the Pro Football Hall of Fame. That same year he became part owner, coach, and general manager of the expansion Cincinnati Bengals in the American Football League. The Bengals named their new stadium after him in 2000 (it's located at One Paul Brown Stadium), and his visage still graces the home page of the team's website. He went 55–59–1 with the Bengals from 1968 to 1975, taking the team to the playoffs in 1970, 1973, and 1975. At that time no other team had qualified for the postseason so early in its history.

Brown continued as general manager of the team until his death from pneumonia at the age of 82 on August 5, 1991. Under his guidance the Bengals reached the Super Bowl twice—in 1982 and 1989—losing to the San Francisco 49ers both times.

In his 1979 autobiography, *PB: The Paul Brown Story* with coauthor Jack Clary, Brown revealed his guiding principle in forming a team: "Everything had to do with people—from properly assessing a man's character, intelligence, and talent to getting him to perform to the best of his ability and in a way that benefited our team. ... I will always be proud, however, of all that our system of football accomplished, not only because we won and left a lasting imprint on the game but because of its effect on the lives of the men who played for us at each level of competition. They are the proofs that our methods and beliefs were correct."

Otto Graham—The Browns' First Superstar

Can you imagine Otto Graham in the Cleveland Orchestra?

The fact of the matter is that the Browns' Hall of Fame quarterback was an accomplished musician. His father was a high school band director in Illinois, and Graham played the piano, violin, French horn, and coronet. He also studied music at Northwestern University. Years after he retired from playing and coaching football, he lamented the fact that he had not kept up with playing the piano, a talent that he felt could make him the life of any party.

Can you imagine Otto Graham in a Cleveland Cavaliers uniform?

Believe it or not, Graham attended Northwestern on a basketball scholarship and became an All-American. He even played with the Rochester Royals of the National Basketball League (the forerunner to the NBA) during their 1946 championship season.

For true Browns fans, imagining Graham in anything but that No. 14 jersey (although he wore No. 60 earlier in his career) is nearly impossible. He is as inseparable from the history of the Browns as Paul Brown himself. Graham was the perfect example of the intelligence, skill, character, and true grit that characterized those early teams.

The funny thing is, Graham, who also played third base, started playing college football only after Northwestern coach Lynn "Pappy" Waldorf spotted him playing intramural football as a freshman. Waldorf inserted Graham at tailback, and, in his very first year, he began to impress observers—including Paul Brown, the coach at Big Ten rival Ohio State.

In his 1979 autobiography, Brown wrote:

The first time I ever saw Otto Graham play football, for instance, was in our 14–7 loss to Pappy Waldorf's Northwestern team—

the only game we lost in 1941. Otto was only a sophomore, playing as a single wing tailback, but against us he looked like anything but a sophomore. In the first quarter, after we had held Northwestern on our 1-yard line and punted from our end zone, he passed to Bud Hasse for a touchdown. We tied the score on Bob Hecklinger's touchdown, but late in the game Otto started to his left as if he were going to run a sweep, and while on the dead run he threw a long pass all the way back to the right side of the field for the winning touchdown. I never forgot Otto's tremendous peripheral vision and his ability to run to his left and then to throw far across the field with such strength and

Quarterback Otto Graham (center), his father (left), and Coach Paul Brown celebrate in the locker room after the Browns won their first NFL title, in 1950.

accuracy. Perhaps it is true you don't forget the players who beat you. I also saw him play football against us twice more and watched him play basketball for Northwestern, and each time I marveled at his athletic ability and his gift of peripheral vision, a must if a passer is going to survey a field and pick out the correct receiver. Not only that, but he could run as well, thus making his passing all the more effective. Years later, Otto was the first player I signed for the Browns because I knew he had all the skills to be a great quarterback.

On March 31, 1945, Graham signed a two-year deal worth $15,000, a huge amount of money in those days. But he proved to be worth every penny. The Browns won 10 division titles and seven championships in Graham's 10 years in the league. He was the best passer in the All-America Football Conference in each of the four years the Browns played in that league, and he was the best passer in the NFL twice. All told he passed for 23,584 yards and 174 touchdowns, and he also scored 276 points on 46 touchdowns. His teams went 114–20–4, and he never missed a game in 10 seasons. He was enshrined in the Pro Football Hall of Fame in 1965 and was named one of the four greatest quarterbacks of all time by the NFL on its 75th anniversary in 1994. (Johnny Unitas, Sammy Baugh, and Joe Montana were the others.)

Graham's performances have stood the test of time. Going into the 2005 NFL season he still ranked 10th in league career passing statistics with an 86.6 quarterback rating (minimum 1,500 passes attempted). He still owns the Browns' highest single-season completion percentage— 64.73 in 1953—and is tied with Brian Sipe for the Browns' record quarterback rating in one game, 158.33 (minimum 15 passes attempted).

TRIVIA

Besides No. 14, what other number did Otto Graham wear with the Browns, and what other position did he play besides quarterback?

Answers to the trivia questions are on pages 159–160.

Graham accomplished that rating in a 31–7 victory over the Chicago Cardinals on October 10, 1954, but he had many games that were remembered more fondly and many that were more important. He completed 22 of 32 passes for 298 yards and four touchdowns in the Browns' 30–28 victory over the Los Angeles Rams for the NFL

By the
NUMBERS

5—Most interceptions in one game (October 17, 1954, at Pittsburgh)

7—300-yard games in career

49—Passes attempted in one game (October 4, 1952, at Pittsburgh)

81—Longest pass play (to Dub Jones, September 30, 1951, vs. San Francisco)

401—Most yards passing in one game (October 4, 1952, at Pittsburgh)

championship on December 24, 1950. He ran for three touchdowns and passed for three more in the Browns' 56–10 victory over Detroit for the NFL championship on December 26, 1954, in what was supposed to be his final game. But Coach Brown persuaded him to return for the 1955 season and paid him the then-astronomical sum of $25,000. In his actual final game Graham ran for two scores and passed for two others in the Browns' 38–14 victory over the Rams for the 1955 NFL championship on December 26, 1955.

After retiring as a player Graham served as coach and later athletics director of the U.S. Coast Guard Academy and the Washington Redskins, where he also served as general manager. Born on December 6, 1921, in Waukegan, Illinois, Graham, who survived colorectal cancer in the 1970s and was diagnosed with Alzheimer's disease in 2001, died of complications from a dissecting aneurysm on December 17, 2003. He was 82 years old.

The Unbeatable Bill Willis

Bill Willis is walking oh-so-slowly through Quicken Loans Arena.

It's not the fact that he's 84 years old, or that he suffered a stroke in 1989, that's slowing him down. It's the fact that every few feet another friend or fan stops him to say hello. The Cleveland Browns Hall of Fame middle guard doesn't get to Cleveland from his home in Columbus all that often any more, so it's a treat for him—and for them—that he agreed to be recognized as one of Ohio's African American sports legends during the Cleveland Cavaliers' Black Heritage Celebration in January 2006.

But with all those hugs and handshakes, it's very slow going. There's no sign of the speed and quickness that became his trademarks and that led the Browns to instruct photographers that they might need to shoot Willis at 1/600th of a second in order to get a clear picture.

For 90 minutes before the Cavaliers game, Willis visited with fellow honorees Oscar Robertson, Harrison Dillard, Edwin Moses, and Ohio State Athletics Director Gene Smith, stopped by a reception for Ohio State alumni, and even signed up for the Ohio State Alumni Association mailing list—as if the university would ever forget how to find an All-American who played on the school's first championship football team, in 1942.

Smith, who was the first African American to be president of the National Association of Collegiate Directors of Athletics, spoke to the alumni group, but not before introducing Willis and Dillard (a graduate of Baldwin-Wallace College) and honoring them for their contributions to the world of sports. "Thank you," Smith told Willis and Dillard. "We would not have what we have today without the battles you fought."

As a round of applause spread through the room, Willis waved his right hand to acknowledge the support. It was impossible not to notice the two substantial rings he was wearing on that hand. There was

A happy group of Browns gather in their locker room after the team's 10th straight win—a 27–16 victory over the Chicago Cardinals at Cleveland Stadium on November 29, 1953. From left to right are tackle coach Weeb Ewbank, tackle Derrell Palmer, quarterback Otto Graham, fullback Harry Jagade, and guard Abe Gibron. Standing behind the group is left half Ken Carpenter. In the front row are Coach Paul Brown (left) and guard Bill Willis. Photo courtesy of Bettmann/CORBIS.

another on his left. Although they appeared to be sizable, they weren't gaudy. "In those days, they didn't have 'bling,'" Willis's son, Clem, noted with a smile.

Willis seemed genuinely thrilled to be asked about the rings. The one on his left pinkie has a No. 1 in diamonds sitting on a red background. After the Buckeyes won the 2002 national championship, Ohio State Coach Jim Tressel presented these rings to the athletes who played on the university's first national championship team, back in 1942. On his right pinkie Willis wears the first Cleveland Browns championship ring, and on his right ring finger he wears his blue and gold Pro Football Hall of Fame ring.

He admits he brings them out only for special occasions. "It would get a little heavy wearing them all the time," he said with a smile.

Clearly this is a special occasion. After watching the first half of the Cavaliers' game against the Indiana Pacers from a suite, Willis makes his way to the court for the halftime ceremony honoring Ohio's black sports legends. The warm reception he receives indicates fans remember the good old days when Willis and the Browns ruled the All-American Football Conference and the National Football League. It has been a long time since the words *Browns* and *ruled* have been used together in a sentence, so the fans have a lot of pent-up cheering to do.

Willis seems touched by the response. Since his wife, Odessa, died in 2003 after 55 years of marriage, Willis rarely returns for Browns functions or agrees to interviews—they bring back too many memories. But for this one night, he has made an exception to talk about how he came to play for Paul Brown.

Even though he grew up in Columbus and became a star athlete at East High School, Willis never really thought about going to Ohio State. "Back then, to go to Ohio State you had to have money, and my folks didn't have money for that school," he recalled.

His high school coach, Ralph Webster, was a graduate of the University of Illinois, and he'd promised to try to get Willis a scholarship there. But when Brown became the coach at Ohio State in 1941, Webster changed his mind. "He told me he thought I'd be much better off at Ohio State," Willis said. "He thought Paul Brown was a very fair individual."

Having grown up in Ohio, Willis knew all about Brown, who had already made a name for himself at Washington High School in Massillon. "I knew he was a great coach," Willis said. "Massillon had the reputation of being a great football program. Massillon was the football center of Ohio. They won state championships and produced outstanding ballplayers."

One of the many things that impressed Willis about Brown was how organized the coach was. His practices were like clockwork, with no wasted time. The results, of course, spoke for themselves. The Buckeyes won the national championship in 1942, when Willis was a sophomore. Willis, who played offensive and defensive tackle and also ran the 60- and 100-yard dashes in track, was an All–Big Ten selection twice and was named an All-American by *Look* magazine and the United Press in 1944.

After graduating from Ohio State, Willis became the athletics director and football coach at Kentucky State, an all-black school in Frankfort. His team lost only two games, but Willis missed playing so much that he decided to have knee surgery in order to try to make the pros. He was heading for Montreal in the Canadian Football League when Brown called and invited him to try out for Cleveland's new All-America Football Conference team in 1946.

TRIVIA

What is Bill Willis's middle name?

Answers to the trivia questions are on pages 159–160.

Stories are still told about how Willis got off the ball so quickly on his first day that he completely disrupted the offense, who screamed that he had to be offside. But he never was. He had perfected the art of moving when the ball was snapped, and in his eight years in pro football, no one ever really figured out how to beat him.

Equal Opportunity

For all the accolades Paul Brown won, for all the championships and honors and innovations he became known for, the one thing he may not have received enough credit for was his commitment to diversity.

In 1946—a year before Branch Rickey signed Jackie Robinson and integrated Major League Baseball—Brown signed Bill Willis and Marion Motley during training camp, making them the first African Americans in the All-America Football Conference and among the first in the modern era of professional football. (The National Football League's Los Angeles Rams signed African Americans Kenny Washington and Woody Strode during the spring of 1946, ending a ban that had been in effect in that league since 1933.) In 1968 Motley, a great blocker and a tremendous runner who excelled in the Browns' trap plays, would become the second African American player named to the Pro Football Hall of Fame. Willis, a middle guard known for his quickness, followed in 1977.

In his autobiography Paul Brown wrote, "I never considered football players black or white, nor did I keep or cut a player just because of his color."

According to Brown's son Mike, president of the Cincinnati Bengals, having black players on the team was never an issue for his father. "The schools in Massillon, where my father grew up, were integrated," Mike Brown said. "He grew up in an integrated world. That doesn't mean there weren't things that today would look odd. But he always felt that people should be judged based on their abilities. He had African American players, as we would call them today—back then they called them *colored*—on his teams when he coached at Massillon."

In his autobiography Brown talked about recruiting Willis to Ohio State.

"Ralph [Webster] was very impressed with the manner in which we treated our black players at Massillon and with our policy of judging them only by their football talent," Brown wrote. "It had really never occurred to me, however, to judge a player in any other manner."

In his book Brown told a story about Willis and Ralph Tyler, the only two black members on the Ohio State track team. In Philadelphia for the Penn Relays, the two were forced to stay in different accommodations and eventually were separated from their teammates, alone and penniless 600 miles from home. When they called him for help, Coach Brown wired them some money and then let the track coach have it for mistreating the athletes.

Running back Marion Motley was one of the first African American players in the modern era of the NFL.

Pro Football Milestones

African American Firsts in Pro Football

First player—Charles Follis, Shelby Athletic Club (1904, although some evidence suggests 1902)

First lineman to win all-league honors—Bill Willis, AAFC Cleveland (1946)

First player to win individual league stats title—Marion Motley, AAFC Cleveland (1946)

First NFL draftee—George Taliaferro, Chicago (1949), but played with AAFC L.A. Dons

First NFL draftee to actually play in the NFL—Wally Triplett, Detroit (1949)

First quarterback—Willie Thrower, Chicago (1953)

First Hall of Famer—Emlen Tunnell, defensive back, New York Giants, Green Bay Packers (inducted in 1967)

First coach—Fritz Pollard, Akron (1921) and Hammond (1925)

First assistant coach—Lowell Perry, Pittsburgh (1957)

First modern-era coach—Art Shell, Los Angeles Raiders (1989)

First general manager—Ozzie Newsome, Baltimore (2002)

First referee—Johnny Grier (1988)

After leaving Ohio State, Brown coached Motley at the Great Lakes Naval Training Center. It was the first time the two were on the same side. Motley had been a star at Canton McKinley, Brown's biggest rival while coaching at Massillon Washington High School.

A few years later, when Brown was putting together his pro team, he knew he wanted Willis and Motley to play for him, but both had quit the game. Willis was a coach at Kentucky State, and Motley was working in a steel mill in Canton—legend has it that when he asked for a tryout, he was told no. Brown always maintained that he waited to sign both players until training camp in an effort to minimize the publicity he knew the move would generate. Three days after Brown signed Willis, he signed Motley, who always figured he was brought along to room with Willis.

According to Mike Brown, Willis and Motley figured into Brown's plans all along:

> When he went to the Browns and started up the team, he immediately understood that he knew where two players were who were better than what he had playing for the Browns. They were both great players, both good, solid guys. A year later, he brought in Horace Gillom, who had played for my dad at Massillon. He was the best player my dad had at Massillon High School. I still think he was the best punter the NFL ever had.
>
> Those three guys roomed together up at Bowling Green, which was where the Browns trained in those days. I was a young kid then, in the late 1940s. I would go up to their room on the second floor. They had the corner room. They were very, very kind to me. We would sit there and play hearts, and the big thing was to put the queen on Marion, because he would squawk and make a stink about it. We all had fun. Those guys were special to me, people I've always had high, high regard for as players and as people.

Mike Brown never thought it was unusual to play cards with a trio of black players.

"They were my heroes," he said. "It didn't seem unusual to me. I was brought up that way, not to think that it should be unusual. It never occurred to me that it was anything different. To this day, it doesn't. It was just something that happened that for me has become a treasured memory."

Of course in some ways signing Willis and Motley (and later Gillom) was the easy part. It was a courageous move, true, but it didn't prevent the inevitable racist encounters. There were the typical insulting epithets and the extra elbows or hits after the whistle, especially for Motley, who often found himself on the bottom of a pile of defenders. The Browns persuaded both men not to react heatedly, because having them thrown out of a

TRIVIA

What Browns record does Horace Gillom still own?

Answers to the trivia questions are on pages 159–160.

23

DID YOU KNOW . . .

That Willis and Motley held a variety of interesting jobs after their playing days were over? Willis worked for the Cleveland Recreation Department and was the director of the Ohio Department of Youth Services. Motley worked for the post office, ran a bar, and coached a women's football team.

game would give their opponents a huge advantage. Instead teammates convinced the two to point out the offenders, who were then taken care of in more subtle ways.

Racism reared its head off the field as well. For instance in 1946 Florida law prevented blacks and whites from competing against each other, so when the Browns had a game at Miami, Brown was forced to tell Willis and Motley they couldn't go.

Wrote Brown in his autobiography, "Both men handled this sensitive situation with great dignity and understanding, however, both then and throughout that season, and they made it easier for other black players to enter professional football."

On another occasion, when a hotel refused to admit Willis and Motley, Brown threatened to pull all his players out and cancel the reservation right then and there. The hotel relented. "I always found that impressive that he was willing to stand up for what he thought in that fashion," Mike Brown said. "To say he was ahead of his time would be an understatement."

Although Paul Brown eventually wound up trading Motley to Pittsburgh in 1955—a move Brown later said was one of the hardest things he'd done in football—he and Willis remained close. Brown invited Willis to join the Bengals. Willis declined, but he still asked Brown to be his presenter when Willis went into the Pro Football Hall of Fame in 1977.

According to Mike Brown, his father never wanted to take credit for helping to integrate football in the modern era:

He talked to me about it. His comment on it was, "People like to give me credit for something I really don't deserve." It never occurred to him that colored, black, African American—take your pick, it has changed over time—players should not be allowed to play. They'd always played for his teams. He didn't much care what someone else might think. He signed them because he thought they should be allowed to play and he thought they were the best players. It was as simple as that. He never gave himself any credit for what he did. He just thought that was the way it should be. He was raised that way. It was how he grew up, the environment he lived in. That was how he conducted himself before coaching the Browns.

One of the interesting little sidelights to that was that one of the people who had a high regard for my father was Branch Rickey. A year after Bill and Marion came to the Browns, Branch Rickey hired Jackie Robinson with the Dodgers. At one time, Branch Rickey tried to hire my father to be the manager for his baseball team when he was running the Pirates in Pittsburgh toward the end of his career. My father didn't think that was what he was. He was right about that.

I'm proud of what he did. I'm proud of why and how he did it. He never even thought that he was deserving credit for that. He thought that was the way it should be. The fact that others didn't do it astonished him. He thought that was stupid. That was how it was.

I'm proud of his role, but he did a lot of things I'm proud of.

Paul Brown established a way of doing things that the Browns continued to follow for years to come. In 1962 Ernie Davis became the first African American player to be taken with the first pick overall in the NFL draft. He was taken by Washington, but the Browns traded for him. In a *Plain Dealer* examination of the Browns' front office in 2003, the team was considerably above the NFL averages for minority vice presidents (17 percent versus 8 percent) and professional administration (20 percent versus 12 percent).

"The NFL would not have had the lowest combined grade in pro sports if it had the hiring record of the Cleveland Browns," Richard Lapchick, director of the Institute for Diversity and Ethics in Sport at the University of Central Florida and author of the semiannual *Racial and Gender Report Card*, told *The Plain Dealer*.

Making an Impression in the NFL: The 1950 Championship Season

The 1950 season was a new beginning for the Cleveland Browns. After Coach Paul Brown's charges dominated the All-America Football Conference so thoroughly for four years that the league disbanded, the team was accepted into the established National Football League along with fellow AAFC alumni Baltimore and San Francisco.

However, they were hardly welcomed. NFL coaches and players looked down on the AAFC and the four-time-champion Browns. One coach went so far as to refer to the Browns as "a basketball team" because they threw the ball so much, which was not the norm back then.

As if to showcase the NFL's superiority—and to teach the Browns how far they had to go—Cleveland's very first game in the league was against the Philadelphia Eagles, who had won the NFL championship in 1949. There was one problem with the plan, however. The Browns refused to play the role of patsy. Instead, quarterback Otto Graham threw for 346 yards and three touchdowns as the Browns hammered the Eagles 35–10 on September 16, 1950, before a crowd of 71,237 in Philadelphia.

"That was the game I remember most," Graham said later. "We were so fired up, we would have played them for a keg of beer or a chocolate milk shake. It was a wonderful, wonderful season."

The rest of the 1950 championship season (recapped here) was certainly one to remember.

September 24—Browns 31, at Baltimore 0. Dub Jones scored on a 60-yard run and Ken Carpenter on a 61-yarder as Cleveland's running game exceeded its passing game for a change. Graham completed just 12 of 23 passes and threw four interceptions.

DID YOU KNOW . . . That the Browns each earned $1,113 for the 1950 championship victory? The losing Rams each took home $636.

October 1—New York Giants 6, Browns 0. Giant Eddie Price's three-yard run seven minutes into the game was the only scoring that would happen as Cleveland stumbled in its home opener. It was the first time in 62 games that the Browns had failed to score. New York coach Steve Owen dropped his ends off the line every time Graham went back to pass. Only 37,647 fans showed up to watch the Browns' first NFL game in Cleveland.

October 7—Browns 30, at Pittsburgh 17. The Browns led 7–3 after Graham's first touchdown run in the first quarter. They broke the game open with two fumble recoveries in the second quarter that resulted in two touchdowns, one by Graham and one by Jones. Another fumble set up Jones's second touchdown, this one in the fourth quarter.

October 15—Browns 34, Chicago Cardinals 24. The Browns trailed 24–10 with six minutes left in the third quarter. But Graham threw two touchdown passes to Dante Lavelli to tie the score, Lou Groza kicked a 19-yard field goal, and Marion Motley ran two yards off right tackle for the Browns' final score.

October 22—At New York Giants 17, Browns 13. The Browns took a 13–3 lead but could not hold it and fell to the Giants for the second time. Unlike the first loss, when Owen had his ends drop back to help cover the Browns' receivers, this time he sent them at Graham, who completed just four passes in the second half.

October 29—Browns 45, Pittsburgh 7. The Browns piled up a team-record 338 rushing yards, led by Motley, who accounted for 188 of them. He scored on runs of 69 and 33 yards. Also joining in the fun was Dopey Phelps, making his first appearance at halfback. Phelps had 13 carries for 87 yards and one touchdown. "We trapped them to death," Brown said later.

November 5—Browns 10, at Chicago Cardinals 7. Jones ran 33 yards for a touchdown on the Browns' first offensive play, and Groza kicked a 17-yard field goal on the second series. The defense held up their end of the bargain as the Browns took over first place in the American Conference.

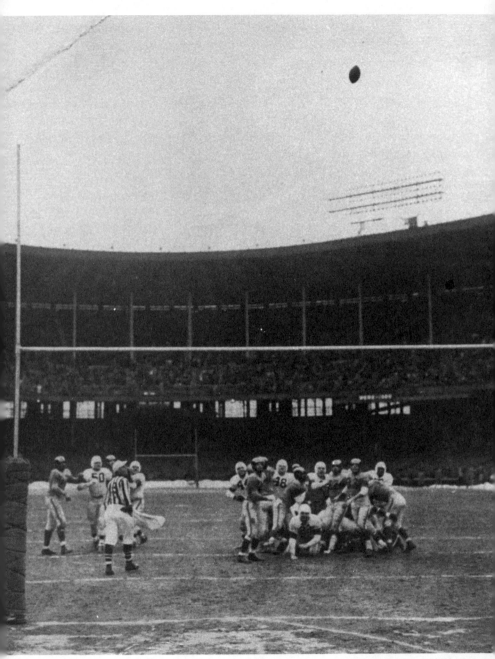

Lou Groza's 16-yard field goal won this game against the Los Angeles Rams and the 1950 NFL title.

November 12—Browns 34, San Francisco 14. Aided by a fumble recovery and an interception, Cleveland scored 17 points in the last four and a half minutes to pull away.

November 19—Browns 20, Washington 14. Dopey Phelps used a key block by Rex Bumgardner to score on an eight-yard run in the closing minutes as the Browns avoided losing to the Redskins, who had lost seven straight coming into the game. "I've been scared to death for a week, because that team is not as bad as its record would have you believe," Brown said. "I'm glad it's over."

December 3—Browns 13, Philadelphia 7. In a rainy game, Warren Lahr returned an interception 30 yards for a touchdown, and Groza kicked two field goals to run his season total to a then–NFL record 12. The Browns did not attempt a pass all game.

December 10—Browns 45, at Washington 21. Graham passed for 321 yards and four touchdowns, two of them to Jones, in the snow.

December 17—Browns 8, New York Giants 3 in the American Conference

TRIVIA

> **Between the two teams, there were 11 future Hall of Famers on the field for the 1950 championship game. Can you name them?**

Answers to the trivia questions are on pages 159–160.

Championship game. Groza kicked a 28-yard field goal with 58 seconds left as the Browns avenged their only two losses of the season in 10-degree weather. Bill Willis saved a touchdown—and probably the game—with a diving stop of Gene Roberts on the Browns' 4-yard line in the fourth quarter.

December 24—Browns 30, Los Angeles Rams 28 in the NFL Championship game. The Browns gave Cleveland fans their first NFL championship—and their fifth title in five years—as a Christmas present. Even better, this one came against the team that had deserted the town five years earlier. Answering all their critics and proving that the team was more than up for the challenge of the NFL, Graham threw four touchdown passes and Groza kicked a 16-yard field goal with 28 seconds left on another brutally cold day.

The Browns trailed 20–28 with eight minutes left before they put together a long drive. Graham completed nine passes to receivers who would catch the ball and then crash into the snowbanks that ringed the field. They pulled within one point on a 14-yard scoring pass from Graham to Bumgardner with 4:35 left and were driving for what they hoped would be the winning score when Graham fumbled on the Rams' 24-yard line with three minutes left. Instead of yelling at Graham, Brown said, "Don't worry, Otts. We're still going to get them." And they did. After the victory before a crowd of 29,751, the fans stormed the field and tore down the goal posts. "This is the gamest bunch of guys in the world," Brown told reporters after the game. "Next to my wife and family, these guys are my life. What a merry Christmas they've made it. ... I never gave up hope. I know this gang too well. I know they never quit. This is the greatest football team a coach ever had. Bless 'em all."

The Man with the Hands: Dante Lavelli

The handsome face was lined but smiling. A jaunty fedora was perched on his head, and black leather gloves covered the hands that made Dante Lavelli famous.

On an unseasonably warm and sunny mid-November afternoon in 2005, the Cleveland Browns were honoring their 1954 and 1955 NFL championship teams before a game against the Miami Dolphins at Cleveland Browns Stadium. Lavelli was one of the first players introduced and, as usual, he received one of the loudest ovations.

He is one of their own. Born in Hudson, Ohio, he attended Ohio State and then signed with the Browns after spending almost three years in the 28th Army Infantry, where he fought in the Battle of the Bulge during World War II. He spent his entire 11-year professional career in Cleveland, and after retiring in 1956, he opened a furniture and appliance store in Rocky River, a Cleveland suburb. Now 83, he still lives in Westlake, another Cleveland suburb.

Inducted into the Hall of Fame in 1975, Lavelli, nicknamed "Gluefingers," is a regular at Browns reunions, golf tournaments, and fund-raisers. He rarely misses a chance to celebrate the history of the team he helped to shape. "It's always good to see original Browns," he said with a smile. (Their numbers are dwindling. For that 2005 reunion, 18 players attended out of the 28 players who were still living at the time.)

As Lavelli wrote in the foreword to *The Cleveland Browns: The Great Tradition*, published in 1999:

> More than 50 years ago, we original Browns established something unique and special in Cleveland—a legacy of success that was rooted in the desire to be the best in the game. Our fans

TOP FIVE

Dante Lavelli's Top Five NFL Seasons

1. 1954—47 catches for 802 yards and seven touchdowns*
2. 1953—45 catches for 783 yards and six touchdowns
3. 1951—43 catches for 586 yards and six touchdowns
4. 1950—37 catches for 565 yards and five touchdowns*
5. 1955—31 catches for 492 yards and four touchdowns*

*Browns won NFL title

throughout Ohio and all over the world soon identified with that success and bonded with us over the years. We owe it all to Paul Brown, who taught us how to play the game, understand the game and respect the game. Unquestionably, Paul Brown was a winner and he surrounded himself with winning players and coaches. ... It's a winning tradition that remains the foundation of Cleveland Browns football.

During Lavelli's 11 seasons with the Browns the team went 119–27–4. In his first 10 seasons they played for the championship every year, winning seven in the All-America Football Conference and the National Football League. As the favorite target of Hall of Fame quarterback Otto Graham, Lavelli was responsible for much of that success. By the end of his career he had caught 386 passes for 6,488 yards and 62 touchdowns. He caught 11 passes in the Browns' 30–28 victory over the Los Angeles Rams (formerly of Cleveland) in the 1950 NFL Championship game in the Browns' first season in the league.

In his autobiography Brown wrote that Lavelli had the best hands he'd ever seen on a receiver. "I can't remember his dropping a single pass during the 11 seasons he played with the Browns—either in a game or in practice," wrote Brown. Lavelli's hands had "an almost liquid softness which seemed to slurp the ball into them."

Lavelli's father was a blacksmith, and the son said he inherited his father's hands. As a kid, Lavelli practiced catching tennis balls or—even harder—Ping-Pong balls. "Did you ever try to catch one?" he asked as the

Browns alumni were assembling to walk onto the field before that 2005 game. "They sail. It gives you touch."

Lavelli was offered a scholarship to Notre Dame, but once Brown went from Massillon's Washington High School to Ohio State, Lavelli wanted to be a Buckeye, too. Brown immediately moved him from halfback to end. An ankle injury cut short Lavelli's sophomore year, and then he was off to fight in World War II. When he came back almost three years later he had offers to play pro basketball or pro baseball. But he went right to Brown's AAFC Browns, jumping at the $500 signing bonus.

He wasted no time in making an immediate impact. He was the top receiver in the AAFC as a rookie and scored the winning touchdown against the New York Yankees in the 1946 AAFC Championship game.

Dante "Gluefingers" Lavelli (right) hauls in another pass.

That Dante Lavelli and Elroy "Crazy Legs" Hirsch were two of the initial organizers of the National Football League Players Association? Formed in 1956, the early goals of the organization were a minimum salary, per diem payments, and continued payments in the event that a player was injured and couldn't play.

Asked what made those early Browns teams so successful, Lavelli didn't hesitate.

"Competition," he said. "There weren't that many jobs. We only had 33 players. When guys came back from Japan and Europe, they didn't have any money. In our first training camp, when the veterans came back, they came with duffel bags. They hitchhiked or took a bus. You had to do what you had to do."

That described Lavelli's approach to football as well. Brown developed the post pattern specifically for Lavelli, but Lavelli would often break the route in order to get open. To make sure Graham always knew where he was, he'd call for the ball in his distinctive high-pitched voice.

That didn't always sit well with Brown, but the coach could hardly disagree with the results. He called Lavelli one of the greatest natural athletes he had ever known and also claimed Lavelli was one of his favorite people.

The 1954 Championship Season

After the Browns won the 1950 NFL Championship by beating the Los Angles Rams 30–28, standout quarterback Otto Graham led them to the championship three more times. But they lost the 1951 title to the Rams 24–17 and the 1952 and 1953 titles to the Detroit Lions 17–7 and 17–16, respectively. At the beginning of the 1954 season Graham informed Coach Paul Brown that this would be Graham's final season.

For a team with a proud history of victory, the previous two years' losses provided the Browns with enough incentive for the 1954 season. But knowing that it would be Graham's last season further inspired the players to give their best. The 1954 championship season (recapped here) would bring happiness to Browns fans for years to come.

September 26—At Philadelphia 28, Browns 10. The Browns, playing without injured linebacker Tom Catlin, lost their opener for just the second time in their nine-year history. Cleveland brought the score to 14–10 in the third quarter, but the Eagles took advantage of Catlin's absence and passed for all four of their touchdowns.

October 10—Browns 31, Chicago Cardinals 7. Graham completed 14 of 18 passes for 266 yards and three touchdowns in the rain. Graham completed his first nine passes and Cleveland scored all its points in the first half.

October 17—At Pittsburgh 55, Browns 27. The Browns actually led 14–7 before the roof fell in. The Steelers scored 27 points in a wild second quarter. Ray Mathews wound up scoring four touchdowns—three of them on passes from Jim Finks. It was Pittsburgh's first victory over Cleveland in nine meetings, and it was a doozy.

October 24—Browns 35, at Chicago Cardinals 3. After stewing about their loss at Pittsburgh for a week, the Browns took it out on the winless

Cardinals to defeat them for the second time that season and the 10th straight time in five years. "We looked considerably better," Brown told reporters after the game.

October 31—Browns 24, New York Giants 14. Graham, ignoring the pain of a bruised shin, ran for two touchdowns and threw a 16-yard scoring pass to Lavelli in the rain and snow.

November 7—Browns 62, Washington 3. Brown actually benched Graham with the Browns leading 13–3 in the second quarter. George Ratterman came in and completed 10 of 11 passes for 208 yards and three touchdowns in the most lopsided victory in the Browns' NFL history. "That Ratterman is a good one," Brown told reporters after the game. "We seemed to need a change of pace and he provided it."

November 14—Browns 39, at Chicago Bears 10. The Browns broke the game open quickly in the third quarter. Zeke Bratkowski muffed a punt from the Bears' end zone, allowing the Browns to start off on the Bears' 28. Six plays later Graham scored on a quarterback keeper. On the Bears' next play from scrimmage Warren Lahr intercepted a Bratkowski pass and returned it for a touchdown.

November 21—Browns 6, Philadelphia 0. The Browns defense came up with a huge goal-line stand after the Eagles had a first down at the Browns' 1-yard line late in the game to preserve the victory and avenge their opening-game loss. The Browns twice stuffed rookie fullback Neil Worden. Mike McCormack then batted down a pass from quarterback Bobby Thomason, breaking a finger on his right hand in the process of knocking down the ball.

November 28—Browns 16, at New York Giants 7. Graham ran for the Browns' only touchdown, and Lou Groza kicked field goals of 18, 10, and 38 yards. The defense allowed the Giants only four yards rushing. New York scored its touchdown on a 48-yard punt return by Herb Johnson.

December 5—Browns 34, at Washington 14. Graham, benched in the first game against the Redskins, completed 13 of 18 passes for 239 yards, and Maurice Bassett rushed for two touchdowns. The Redskins took a 7–0 lead, easing Brown's fears that his team would be too lackadaisical after the easy victory a month earlier. After the game Redskins tackle Dave Sparks of Lorain, Ohio, died of a heart attack while dining with friends.

Chet Hanulak (carrying ball) helped the Browns win a title as a rookie in 1954.
Photo courtesy of Diamond Images.

That as big as the Browns championship run was, it had to share headlines in 1954 with the murder trial of Dr. Sam Sheppard, who was accused of killing his wife, Marilyn? He was found guilty and spent 10 years in prison before the U.S. Supreme Court overturned his conviction. He was acquitted in a retrial in 1966. The case became the basis for the television program *The Fugitive*, which was later made into a movie starring Harrison Ford, Tommy Lee Jones, and Sela Ward.

December 12—Browns 42, Pittsburgh 7. Rookie Chet Hanulak got his first start and scored three touchdowns as the Browns won the Eastern Conference for a record fifth time, setting up a rematch with the Detroit Lions for the NFL championship. Hanulak, starting for Ray Renfro, who missed the game with an injured knee, finished with 12 carries for 94 yards. So thoroughly did the Browns dominate that Graham played only the first half after Cleveland built a 28–0 lead.

December 19—Lions 14, Browns 10. On his 28th birthday, Detroit quarterback Bobby Layne threw an 11-yard touchdown pass to Earl "Jug" Girard with 50 seconds left in a game that had been postponed because of the World Series. The Browns had taken a 10–7 lead in the third quarter on a 43-yard field goal by Groza, who was announced as the league's Most Valuable Player by *The Sporting News*.

December 26—Browns 56, Lions 10. Graham, who was expected to retire after the game, ran for three touchdowns and passed for three more as the Browns won their second NFL championship and their sixth league title overall since 1946. It was the first time Graham and the Browns had beaten the Lions. It was the second-highest-scoring playoff game in NFL history, surpassed only by the Chicago Bears' 73–0 victory over the Washington Redskins in 1940.

"The finest football team I've ever coached on a given day," Coach Paul Brown told reporters after the game. Detroit coach Buddy Parker did not disagree. "I saw it, but still hardly can believe it," said Parker.

Lou Groza:
Always There in the Clutch

Of all the great players who have worn the orange and brown, of all those who contributed to the legendary success of the Cleveland Browns, none did it longer or better than Lou Groza. The Smithsonian once displayed his shoes, and college football's best kicker wins an award in his name every year.

As the Browns' place-kicker from day one of their inception in 1946, Groza—nicknamed "the Toe" by a clever Cleveland sportswriter—earned the undying respect of Paul Brown, who was one of the first coaches to realize the strategic importance of having a great place-kicker. "I know that Lou won more games in clutch situations with his kicking than any player in the game's history," Brown wrote in his autobiography.

Groza's performance is so dominant that despite the fact that his four seasons (and 259 points) in the All-America Football Conference aren't even counted, he still ranks number one in Browns history in years of service (17 in the National Football League) and scoring (1,349 points during 17 NFL seasons on 234 field goals and 641 points after touchdowns). He even scored one touchdown, on a pass from Graham, in a 45–21 victory over Washington on December 10, 1950. He scored at least one point in 107 consecutive games, another team record.

At 6'3" and 235 pounds he was hardly the prototypical kicker. He also played left tackle on offense from 1946 to 1959, making the All-NFL team as a tackle six times, and the fact of the matter is that when he was inducted into the Pro Football Hall of Fame, it was as a tackle, an honor of which he was extremely proud.

How important was Groza to the success of the franchise? The address of the team's training facility in Berea is 76 Lou Groza Boulevard.

TRIVIA

What two numbers did Lou Groza wear while with the Browns?

Answers to the trivia questions are on pages 159–160.

Groza grew up in Martins Ferry, Ohio, on the West Virginia border near Wheeling. His parents owned a tavern. His brother Frank taught him how to kick a football, but he excelled at basketball and baseball as well. He often bragged about the free throws he made to help his basketball team win a state title. As a result, he was named the most valuable player in the state basketball tournament.

With his athletic ability and the fact that he was a member of the National Honor Society, Groza attracted a lot of attention from colleges. He was very impressed with Notre Dame, but when it came time to choose, he wanted to stay closer to home and play for the legendary Paul Brown at Ohio State.

He never really got the chance. Though he impressed the coach with his 70-yard kickoffs and his 40- and 50-yard field goals for the freshman team, freshmen weren't eligible for Brown's varsity team, and long before he became a sophomore he was sent off to the Pacific with the 96th Infantry in World War II. He served as a surgical technician, so he saw the horrors of the war up close and on a daily basis.

Groza was shocked when an offer from Brown arrived in the mail: $500 a month until the war was over and $7,500 to play for the Browns upon his return to the States. He never got to play for Brown in college, but the coach wanted to make sure he had Groza's services in the pros. He was the second player the coach signed after quarterback Graham.

Groza played in 275 games with the Browns, 216 of them in the National Football League, and there was scarcely one of them in which he didn't figure in the outcome. With 28 seconds left he kicked the winning field goal that gave the Browns their first NFL championship in their first season in the league in 1950. He missed the 1960 season with a back injury, but new owner Art Modell talked him into coming back in 1961, and he played through the 1967 season, enjoying his most prolific season in 1964, when he scored 115 points. He was the only one of the original Browns to play in every one of the team's championship games.

After he retired Groza ran a successful insurance business, and he was a fixture at Browns reunions and alumni functions. Slowed in his

Lou "the Toe" Groza considered himself a lucky man.

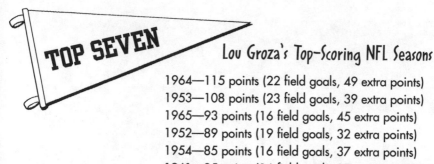

TOP SEVEN — Lou Groza's Top-Scoring NFL Seasons

1964—115 points (22 field goals, 49 extra points)
1953—108 points (23 field goals, 39 extra points)
1965—93 points (16 field goals, 45 extra points)
1952—89 points (19 field goals, 32 extra points)
1954—85 points (16 field goals, 37 extra points)
1961—85 points (16 field goals, 37 extra points)
1963—85 points (15 field goals, 40 extra points)

later years by back and hip surgeries and Parkinson's disease, he died of a heart attack on November 29, 2000, at the age of 76.

Before his death Groza spoke to author Alan Natali for his book *Brown's Town: 20 Famous Browns Talk Amongst Themselves*. He made it clear that he was happy with his life and that he felt he owed it all to Brown. Wrote Groza:

Where would I have been if he hadn't have seen me playing basketball in Martins Ferry and Columbus. That's where I first got the idea that I could be something.

It's hard to believe I've been retired for so long. It's been a great life. I've been lucky. I look back, and I feel fortunate to have survived a war and all the things that can happen to you when you play ball. I look back and ask, How lucky can a guy get? To play his whole career in one city for a winner and enjoy the success we had. It makes for a very happy existence.

The 1955
Championship Season

The post–Otto Graham era—and the Browns' defense of their 1954 National Football League title—started badly. The team lost five of six exhibition games. Things were looking so bleak that Coach Brown called Graham and asked him to come out of his brief retirement. As an enticement Brown offered Graham a salary of $25,000, more than any player in the league was then making.

The 1955 championship season (recapped here) was an amazing follow-up to the team's stellar performance in 1954.

September 25—Washington 27, Browns 17. Washington's plucky little quarterback Eddie LeBaron threw for two touchdowns and ran for a third as the Redskins upset the Browns, who lost their season opener for the second straight year. "The little man beat us personally," Brown said of LeBaron after the game. Graham, who had reported to the team only three weeks earlier, struggled in the first half and did not play in the second. "There is no doubt that Graham's late arrival made it difficult to get a good organization out there," Brown told reporters after the game.

October 2—Browns 38, at San Francisco 3. The 49ers, who had beaten the Browns 17–14 during the exhibition season, took a 3–0 lead in this game, but that was the only scoring they would do all afternoon. The Browns broke the game open with 17 points in the second quarter en route to a 24–3 lead at halftime. San Francisco quarterback Y. A. Tittle completed only seven of 15 passes for 57 yards, and the 49ers offense managed a total of only 139 yards. It was the worst loss ever for the 49ers at home and the first time since 1950 that they failed to score a touchdown.

October 9—Browns 21, Philadelphia 17. The Browns trailed 17–14 with about three minutes left. But Graham saved the day, driving the

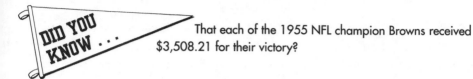

team 87 yards in 11 plays, running 60 of those yards himself before throwing a five-yard touchdown pass to Dante Lavelli with 1:13 left.

October 16—Browns 24, at Washington 14. Fullback Ed "Big Mo" Modzelewski scored twice as the Browns avenged their season-opening loss. However, the Browns lost safety Tommy James with a left knee injury on the first play from scrimmage.

October 23—Browns 41, Green Bay Packers 10. The Browns gained a whopping 454 yards on offense, including 250 yards passing, but suffered two more key injuries. Linebacker Sam Palumbo suffered a dislocated right shoulder. He was taken to the hospital during the game and returned to the sideline with his arm in a sling. Modzelewski also suffered a slight shoulder separation.

October 30—Browns 26, at Chicago Cardinals 20. Cleveland pulled out to a 21–6 lead in the pouring rain before the Cardinals rallied for two touchdowns in the second half. But the defense stopped Chicago when it counted. Chuck Noll, who had scored on a safety early in the third quarter, picked off an interception late in the game to preserve the victory.

November 6—Browns 24, New York Giants 14. Quarterback George Ratterman replaced Graham, who had suffered a slight concussion after being tackled in the second quarter. The game was a tale of two halves. New York dominated the first half, compiling 217 yards to Cleveland's 90. The tables were turned in the second half, when Cleveland amassed 227 yards to New York's five. Ratterman scored the game's final touchdown on a four-yard bootleg play that fooled the Giants on fourth down.

November 13—At Philadelphia 33, Browns 17. The Browns totally dominated the first quarter, putting up 17 points. Unfortunately, they still had to play three more quarters. Philadelphia rallied for 17 points in the fourth quarter to snap Cleveland's winning streak at six games. More injuries plagued the Browns. Cornerback Don Paul had a charley horse while safety John Petitbon, who had replaced James, suffered a rib injury. "How well we recover from our injuries will decide whether we can stay in contention," Brown said after the game.

November 20—Browns 41, Pittsburgh 14. The Steelers, hampered by injuries to Lynn Chandnois and Bill McPeak, didn't put up much of a fight in this game. Safety Ken Konz scored on an interception return for Cleveland.

November 27—Browns 35, at New York Giants 35. Each team scored 14 points in a wild fourth quarter, but the Browns' bid to score 17 and win the game ended when Giants tackle Ray Krouse blocked a 21-yard field-goal attempt by Lou Groza in the closing seconds. Krouse and Ray Beck also blocked a 27-yard field-goal attempt by Groza in the second quarter.

December 4—Browns 30, at Pittsburgh 7. With this victory the Browns claimed their 10th straight division or conference title. Groza kicked the first of his three field goals of the day—a 16-yarder—with 2:37 gone in the game, and the Browns rolled from there. Groza added 22- and 26-yard field goals. The defense picked off four interceptions and

Chicago's Ollie Matson (No. 33) is tackled by a gang of Browns during the first quarter of Cleveland's 35–24 victory on December 11, 1955. Photo courtesy of Bettmann/CORBIS.

TRIVIA

Exactly 232 of the 234 passes attempted by the Browns in 1955 were thrown by Otto Graham (185) and George Ratterman (47). Who threw the other two?

Answers to the trivia questions are on pages 159–160.

limited Pittsburgh, which had entered the game as the NFL's top passing team, to just 97 yards passing.

December 11—Browns 35, Chicago Cardinals 24. Graham threw for 182 yards and three touchdowns as the Browns kept their winning streak against Chicago teams intact. (They had never lost to a Chicago team since their inception in the All-America Football Conference in 1946.)

December 26—Browns 38, Los Angeles Rams 14. The Browns won their second straight NFL championship and their third since joining the league in 1950. It was their seventh championship since their inception in the All-America Football Conference in 1946. Graham, whose retirement was guaranteed this time, made sure his finale was grand, running for two touchdowns and passing for two more in a rematch of the 1950 championship game. The defense picked off seven interceptions, six of them by Norm Van Brocklin, who was finally benched in the third quarter.

Jim Brown:
A Hero on the Field,
a Star on the Big Screen

There may be no player so closely identified with the Cleveland Browns as legendary running back Jim Brown. Although the franchise was named after equally legendary coach and founder Paul Brown, there is little doubt that there were children growing up in the 1960s who thought the team was actually named after its biggest star.

While Otto Graham, Dante Lavelli, Marion Motley, Lou Groza, Bill Willis, and others were stars in their own rights on Browns teams that achieved unparalleled success, Brown's greatness played out on a larger stage at a time when the National Football League was using its national television exposure to become the giant it is today.

Brown played nine memorable seasons for Cleveland from 1957 to 1965 and was named the league's Most Valuable Player in 1958 and 1965. His rushing average (5.22 yards per carry) remains an NFL record. In 1971 at the age of 35 he became the second-youngest player inducted into the Hall of Fame (he was one year older than Chicago's Gale Sayers).

Brown made the Pro Bowl nine times and was named All-Pro in eight of them, losing out only in 1962. That happened to be one of the two seasons he failed to rush for 1,000 yards. He had 942 yards as a rookie in 1957, good enough to earn the NFL's Rookie of the Year award, and 996 yards in 1962, when he lost some yardage late in a game at San Francisco, again preventing him from reaching the 1,000-yard mark. He led the league in rushing eight times.

Brown still holds the Browns records for combined net yards in a career (15,459), most yards rushing in a career (12,312), most points in one season (126), career touchdowns (126), career rushing touchdowns (106), consecutive games scoring a touchdown (10), most 1,000-yard seasons (seven), most rushing yards in a season (1,863), most rushing

Running back Jim Brown, making his way past some Eagles for his 106th career touchdown, may have been the best ever.

yards in a game (237), and most rushing attempts in a career (2,359). His No. 32 was retired by the team.

Is it any wonder then that Brown is a marked man when he strolls the sideline at Cleveland Browns Stadium on a cold and snowy December afternoon before a game against the Jacksonville Jaguars? He is besieged by fans asking for photographs (which he obliges) and autographs (which he declines). Fans who can get close enough shake his hand or pat him on the back. Fans farther away call his name, wave and clap, and give him a thumbs-up. Still close to 6'2" as he nears the age of 70, he looks strong and fit and not too far away from his playing weight of 232 pounds. Interestingly, he is wearing a Nike warm-up suit featuring the LJ23 insignia of the Cavaliers' LeBron James.

Asked if being on a Browns sideline in December 2005 was any different from being on a Browns sideline in December 1965, when the team played at cavernous Cleveland Municipal Stadium, Brown replied:

There's really no difference. The weather is the weather. The feeling is always about the smell of football, the feel of football, the purpose, the different way you have to run because it's going to be a little slippery, hoping that it doesn't get too wet, knowing the ball is going to be slippery and preparing yourself to perform and take all those things into account. It is a Cleveland day. It's football weather, Cleveland weather. Even though the stadium is different, we're used to this now. It's in the same place, basically, down by the lake.

It's great to be here. I guess my real feeling is that it's great to be a part of what's going on right now and to be able to impart anything that would be helpful. It's almost the same desire to win. I don't like to lose. I don't like to see bad performances. I love to see the attitudes of young players. I love to see an organization that has a lot of real fine young men on the team, young men of character, rather than a bunch of buffoons. There are a lot of thoughts that go through my mind.

Brown's official title is listed as executive adviser. The team press guide says his role is to help build relationships with players and to enhance the NFL's wide range of sponsored programs through the Browns' player programs department. He makes frequent trips to Cleveland, although he lives in Los Angeles, where he is still active in his Amer-I-Can program, which teaches self-help principles to gang members and ex-convicts.

Asked why he decided to take a formal position with the Browns at this stage in his life, Brown answered that it was his relationship with Randy Lerner, who took over ownership of the team when his father, Al, died in 2002. Of Lerner, Brown said:

I bonded with him before his father died, recognized he had a great mind and was a great humanitarian. I remember one particular conversation I had with him while everybody else was talking to his father. I recognized that this kid had been groomed beautifully with his educational background, his interest in art, his level of intelligence, and the fact that he was the son of a famous man. I didn't know his father was going to die. That was a tragedy. But we had already formed our bond.

It has been two years since he came out to L.A. to meet with me and reach back for a lot of the history, a lot of the tradition. He sort of needed my assistance with reorganizing. I did it strictly because of him and his family. They're all rooted in Cleveland tradition. He was now the owner and had a great attitude. He knew a lot about me. People don't usually research me the way he did. He read some books nobody else read, including a particular book on me called *Jim* written by James Toback. I felt like I was part of the family again. My presence was desired. Nobody wants to be anywhere they're not wanted.

Was there actually a time that the great Jim Brown felt unwanted by the Cleveland Browns?

"Oh, yeah—the regime that left," he said, referring to fired team president Carmen Policy and his administration. "I didn't come to one game the year before last. It wasn't that anybody was negative. No one did anything wrong. It just seemed they were developing a different concept of what the Browns were. It was like, 'Are we San Francisco or are we Cleveland?'"

By the
NUMBERS

Jim Brown's Rushing Totals by Season

942—1957

1,527—1958

1,329—1959

1,257—1960

1,408—1961

996—1962

1,863—1963

1,446—1964

1,544—1965

Technically, there was another time the Browns didn't know if they wanted Brown. When it came to the NFL draft in 1957 the team really was in need of a quarterback to replace Graham, who had retired after winning the NFL championship in 1955. John Brodie, Paul Hornung, and Len Dawson were available heading into the draft. The first two were taken immediately, and the Browns lost a coin flip with Pittsburgh for the fifth pick. The Steelers took Dawson. Paul Brown selected Jim Brown as the proverbial "best player available." Even if Jim Brown was the Browns' second choice, Paul Brown paid him a $12,000 salary with a $3,000 bonus—the most ever for a Browns rookie.

By the time he came to the Browns, Jim Brown already had made quite a name for himself. He was born February 17, 1936, on St. Simons Island on the Georgia coast. He barely knew his father, a gambler named Swinton "Sweet Sue" Brown, and when he was just two years old his mother moved without him to Long Island, New York, where she had a job as a maid. Brown was raised by his great-grandmother, his grandmother, and his aunt. When he was eight his mother got a job as a domestic in Manhasset, New York. She was provided with an apartment, so she sent for her son, who developed into a popular sports star at Manhasset High School, where he was also voted chief justice of the school's supreme court. During his senior year he averaged 15

TRIVIA

Which five sports did Jim Brown play in high school?

Answers to the trivia questions are on pages 159–160.

IF ONLY . . . Jim Brown had not retired before the 1966 season, the Browns might have won more NFL titles. They failed to make the playoffs in 1966, although Leroy Kelly did gain 1,141 yards. Would Brown have made a difference? How about in 1967, when the Browns lost 30–6 to the L.A. Rams in the Playoff Bowl? Or in 1968, when they lost 34–0 to the Baltimore Colts in the NFL Championship game? Or in 1969, when they lost 27–7 to the Minnesota Vikings in the NFL Championship game?

Regardless of what might have been, Brown said he never second-guessed his decision to retire. "It's one of the best things I ever did," he said. "That's looking at the big picture. Immediate gratification is a mistake that a lot of people make. The big picture means your legacy will last forever if you treat it properly. If you abuse it based on greediness trying to get immediate gratification, it will come back to haunt you because you'll have to qualify your work. Let your work qualify itself. You'll have no argument when your legacy is correct."

yards per carry in football and 38 points per game in basketball. He played baseball well enough that the New York Yankees offered him a tryout.

Brown garnered 45 scholarship offers but decided to attend Syracuse University, which was not among the 45. The only black player on the football team, he was fifth string as a sophomore and broke into the starting lineup only after a series of injuries to other players. A couple of games later he wowed fans and teammates alike with a 54-yard touchdown run, finishing with 150 yards rushing. He started every game for the rest of his college career and was named an All-American as a senior. He was also a star lacrosse player.

Paul Brown may have had some issues with Jim Brown concerning his attitude and approach to practice and blocking, but the coach could not help but marvel at Brown's talent. He called him a once-in-a-lifetime player who became the best running back ever to play professional football. In his autobiography, Paul Brown said of Jim Brown:

The keys to his success were that rare combination of strength and speed we had noticed before drafting him. He was not a knee-pumping type of runner but had the ability to shuffle laterally if a hole closed, and once he found an opening, his acceleration caused tacklers just to bounce off him. There were tacklers who thought they had him, but Jim had the unusual ability of allowing one of his legs to go limp, and when the tackler relaxed, he surged forward again, ripping apart the man's grip. Jim was also a most determined runner, who would have been even greater had he played on today's artificial surfaces. Though he played half his games on the heavy natural field in Cleveland, it never bothered him because he had such great balance; his feet were never far off the ground when he ran, so he was very difficult to knock down. Another key was the unusual muscle structure in his upper thighs that generated his power.

Paul Brown was gone by the time Jim Brown retired. Owner Art Modell, who bought the team in 1961, fired the beloved coach after the 1962 season. Though Modell had befriended Jim Brown, he still threatened to fine Brown when he was late to training camp in 1966 because filming for his movie, *The Dirty Dozen*, was taking longer than expected. So Brown wrote to Hal Lebovitz of *The Plain Dealer* to announce his retirement.

Forty years later, Jim Brown has no regrets. He still calls the 1964 championship the biggest thrill of his football career:

Absolutely. One of the things about it was that it was a total team effort. I tell people today that football's the ultimate team sport because Frank Ryan, Jim Brown, Paul Warfield, and Gary Collins didn't play one down of defense. So the great Johnny Unitas and Raymond Berry and Lenny Moore and John Mackey were shut down. Since we [on the offense] didn't play any defense, that's the greatest illustration of a team effort. Frank threw three touchdown passes. Gary caught three of them. The line blocked beautifully for me. The defense shut out an all-star team [Baltimore in a championship game in 1964]. That lives forever for us. When we come back together, everybody feels valuable. It wasn't just one person that did it.

How does Brown describe his relationships with Coach Brown and Modell? Echoing the comments Paul Brown made in his autobiography, Jim Brown said:

DID YOU KNOW . . . That after retiring from the Browns, Jim Brown appeared in 32 movies? *The Dirty Dozen* and *Ice Station Zebra* were the best known.

I had good relationships with them. I'm an independent thinker, so I've always had differences. But I had great respect for both of them in their own ways. I thought Paul's only mistake was that he got a little outdated. He didn't want to make the changes that were necessary to do what we had to do in the modern era. But he was a great organizer and a great coach. Then he got too conservative.

Art is Art. Art is a businessman of a certain kind. He and I could always talk. He was Ozzie Newsome's guru. He created a lot of positions on the Ravens for African American executives. So behind the scenes, you have to look at what's truly valued. Leaving Cleveland was a disaster. But from what I understood it was either doing that or declaring bankruptcy. Later on you could see that his economics weren't together because he had to make a deal and he's not an owner any more. So he left [the game] himself based upon his bad management of the economic situation.

Brown has had some off-field problems himself. In 1965 a Cleveland jury found him not guilty of assault and battery on an 18-year-old girl. Charges were dropped in a few other much-publicized incidents later in his life.

But none of those affected his stature in Cleveland. Randy Lerner felt Brown was the perfect person to serve as a living link for current players to the proud history of the Browns franchise. Young players or those who don't stay with a team for more than a year or two at a time may not realize exactly what playing for the Browns means.

"They might be less familiar, but they get a feeling when you maintain your history," Brown said. "There's a feeling of value and less commerciality in this day of commerciality. So they might not know it technically, but when they see the 1954 or '55 championship teams come back, or the '64 championship team come back, when individuals like [former Browns guard] John Wooten are interfacing, they get a sense of the history, and they should."

One of Brown's first acts after taking the job was brokering a compromise between the Browns and running back Reuben Droughns, who was threatening to hold out after being traded to the Browns from Denver before the 2005 season. Brown persuaded Droughns to come in and prove himself and told Lerner that he'd have to enhance Droughns's contract if he proved himself on the field. Lo and behold, Droughns became the first Browns running back to rush for more than 1,000 yards in 20 years.

Ironically, Brown never put much stake on the 1,000-yard milestone:

I never talked about 1,000 yards because I never used it as my yardstick. That doesn't mean I don't appreciate the fact that Reuben will get 1,000, because it has been 20 years. It's very inspirational for people. The standard is one that can have a value, or have no value. I gave it no value. Because for 12 games, 1,000 yards is not a 100-yard average.

Now it's better in this situation because Reuben stood up and re-created an interest in our running game. Reuben just brought an attitude with his ability. The combination of ability and attitude is a very good thing for our running game.

Perhaps—but not quite as good as Brown was. It would take a very special player indeed to match what he brought to the team.

The Controversial
Art Modell

Even now, 10 years and 400 miles removed from Cleveland and out of football entirely, there is no mistaking the joy in Art Modell's voice when he talks about purchasing the Cleveland Browns in 1961. "I was never happier than the day I closed that deal," Modell said in a telephone interview from his home outside Baltimore.

With the exception of Dallas's Jerry Jones, there may never have been another man who was more thrilled to own a National Football League team. Modell loved everything about being an owner—hobnobbing with the movers and shakers and the politicians and celebrities, kibitzing with players and coaches, shooting the breeze with the media. He was in his element.

"I became owner and went to my first practice," Modell said. "I was standing behind the huddle as they were going through their routine. I couldn't believe what I was watching. Here I'm watching the Cleveland Browns owned by Art Modell. I was like a kid in a candy store."

Life had not always been so sweet. Modell went through many hard times before he came to Cleveland. Growing up in Brooklyn, Modell's father, George, had a successful appliance store, and the Modells were fairly well-to-do. But the family lost everything in the stock market crash of 1929 and the Great Depression, forcing his father to become a traveling salesman. George Modell died on a business trip to Austin when Art Modell was just 14 years old. Art dropped out of high school and took a job in a shipyard to help support his family, eventually earning his diploma by going to night school. He enlisted in the air force at the age of 18. After World War II, he decided to pursue a career in television and eventually switched to advertising, a background that would serve him well once he became an NFL owner.

IF ONLY . . .

Art Modell had not moved the team, Bill Belichick might have led the Browns to three Super Bowl championships in four years, as he did the New England team.

In 1960 Modell heard through the grapevine that an NFL team might be for sale. He was intrigued long before he even knew which team it was. "As an old sports fan of baseball, football, and hockey, my dream was to own a team," he said. "This tip came along through a theatrical agent. He heard a team could be bought. I thought it was the New York Giants, which was my hometown team. Then we met with some people and they said it was the Cleveland Browns. I was overwhelmed. The next day I went out with my attorneys to Cleveland to start the discussions, which eventually led to the purchase at a very high price. It was very costly, but it was very rewarding for me."

The team was sold for an unheard-of $3.9 million to the 35-year-old Modell. "That 35-year-old man didn't have a nickel to his name," Modell recalled, laughing. "But I had creditworthiness. I had a tremendous reputation amongst the bankers in New York, and eventually the bankers in Cleveland. This one banker, George Herzog of Union Commerce Bank, extended me enough credit to buy the team and even gave me some personal credit so I could buy more stock in the team. It was a magnificent gesture. He said, 'Art, let me tell you this. I've been in banking for 60 years. I don't bet on balance sheets. I bet on people.' I was impressed with that."

Modell had spent his life working, but he had no idea how to be an NFL owner. "I had to be self-taught, a very costly experience for me," he admitted. "I learned the business quickly and adapted myself. I was in the office at 6:30 or 7:00 o'clock in the morning, worked until after dinner, had a sandwich brought in. They were 18- or 19-hour days. I did it every day for years. I was not married. I had an apartment on the west side of Cleveland. My whole life was wrapped up in my work. My work was to see the Cleveland Browns become the best there was in professional football. We were for a while."

Early in his tenure Modell found himself at odds with two of the biggest legends in the history of the Browns franchise—Coach Paul Brown and star running back Jim Brown.

Art Modell (far left) rubbed elbows with (from left) Pete Rozelle, Tex Schramm, Milt Woodard, and Lamar Hunt.

Paul Brown was used to running the show, and he didn't care for Modell's hands-on approach. In his autobiography, Paul Brown referred to his two years under Modell as "the darkest period of my life." Modell certainly never imagined he would have to fire the great Paul Brown, the only coach the team had ever had, but after the 1962 season that was exactly what he did.

"One of the reasons I bought the Browns, or was intrigued by the Browns, was that he was around," Modell said of Paul Brown. "He was an icon, the greatest coach in football. I was so thrilled to have a team he was running. He sort of turned on me after a while. He didn't like me asking too many questions. They were sincere questions—not to undermine him. Anyhow, it came to an end and I had to ask him to leave."

As for Jim Brown, Modell was closer to his star running back than he was to any other player at the time. However, by 1966 Brown was pursuing his acting career. He had intended to return for the season, but when filming for *The Dirty Dozen* ran long, he failed to show for training camp. Modell threatened to fine him, and Brown opted to retire, writing a letter to *The Plain Dealer*'s Hal Lebovitz to announce it.

"Jim Brown was my guy for a long time," Modell said. "He was the greatest football player I've ever seen. We had a good relationship. Then he went his way and I went my way. You just can't live in the past. You've got to live for today."

Asked if he was surprised that Brown retired in the prime of his career, Modell answered, "I was surprised and angry. He said he was coming back to training camp. Then he called a press conference in London and announced his retirement [after sending a letter to Lebovitz]. That was it. I was not a happy camper."

Overall, there were more good times than bad during Modell's time in Cleveland. Certainly one of the best—next to his marriage to actress Patricia Breslin, anyway—was winning the 1964 National Football League championship. "It was the thrill of a lifetime until we won the Super Bowl here in Baltimore [after the 2000 season]," Modell said. "When you win the big enchilada, it's something you'll never forget. ... We were just a simple little game in Cleveland. We had nationwide TV and a sold-out crowd. The place went wild when we won that game. We almost had a riot on the field. I will never forget it. You never forget your first kiss."

Modell presided over the Browns' move to the American Football Conference when the NFL merged with the American Football League in 1970. He volunteered for the first *Monday Night Football* game that same season. He served as chairman of the NFL's broadcast committee for 35 years and was president of the league from 1967 to 1970, positions that led to his being nominated for the Pro Football Hall of Fame.

He was not afraid to try new things. He staged concerts along with games and created preseason doubleheaders, which he called a "smash hit." "They were the social event in Cleveland that time of year," Modell recalled. "It was a very rewarding and gratifying experience to see that thing take off as it did."

He remembered one doubleheader in particular. On the morning of the game someone phoned in a bomb threat, claiming that a device

By the NUMBERS

Coaches under Art Modell (by Season)

1961–62—Paul Brown

1963–70—Blanton Collier

1971–74—Nick Skorich

1975–77—Forrest Gregg

1977—Dick Modzelewski (interim)

1978–84—Sam Rutigliano

1984–88—Marty Schottenheimer

1989–90—Bud Carson

1990—Jim Shofner (interim)

1991–95—Bill Belichick

planted in Cleveland Municipal Stadium would explode at 10:00 PM. Modell called in the FBI, who swept the place and found nothing. That night Modell was sitting in the press box with Jim Finks and Vince Lombardi. "I kept one eye on the clock and one eye on the field," he said. "I couldn't take my eye off that clock. As the hands approach 10:00, our press box attendant decides to go out. The wind took the door and slammed it shut. We leaped so high, we nearly ended up in the upper deck. Nothing else happened, fortunately."

For all those good times, there were bad times, too. Health problems. Heartbreaking losses with nicknames like "Red Right 88," "The Drive," and "The Fumble." There was the unceremonious dumping of local hero Bernie Kosar. But all those paled in comparison to Modell's 1995 announcement that he was moving the team to Baltimore. Outraged Cleveland fans bombarded the offices of the commissioner and the other NFL owners. A compromise allowed Modell to move his franchise but mandated that he leave the Browns' name and history in Cleveland, where a new team would begin play in 1999 after a three-year hiatus.

The 1964 Championship Season

The Browns were suffering through the worst playoff drought in their existence.

This was a team that had played in a championship game in each of its first 10 years in existence, winning four titles in the All-America Football Conference and three more in the National Football League. After winning back-to-back championships in 1954 and 1955 the Browns recorded their first losing season in 1956, when they finished 5–7 and missed the playoffs for the first time.

The good news? Their record put them in position to draft fullback Jim Brown out of Syracuse. With Brown on board, the Browns lost the 1957 NFL championship 59–14 to Detroit. They lost a 1958 playoff game 10–0 to the New York Giants. They failed to make the playoffs in 1959, and then they lost the Playoff Bowl to the Lions again, 17–16, after the 1960 season. They missed the playoffs in 1961 and 1962. Then new owner Modell fired Coach Brown and replaced him with Blanton Collier. With Collier the team lost the Playoff Bowl 40–23 to the Green Bay Packers after the 1963 season.

It had been nine years since the Browns finished on top of the National Football League. For a team with the proud history of the Browns, that was way too long. But the 1964 championship season (recapped here) would put the Browns back where they belonged—at the head of the class.

September 13—Browns 27, at Washington 13. In a steady rain the Browns spotted the Redskins a 10–0 lead in the second quarter. But Cleveland scored 20 straight points and built a 20–10 lead in the third quarter. The rain bothered both teams. Washington had four fumbles, while Cleveland had three interceptions.

Brown Gary Collins (No. 86) leaps for the first of his three touchdowns on passes thrown by Frank Ryan against the Colts. Defending on the play is Colt Jim Welch (No. 46). Photo courtesy of Bettmann/CORBIS.

September 20—Browns 33, St. Louis 33. A crowd of 76,945 for the home opener went away disappointed. Gary Collins caught a 43-yard pass to set up a touchdown run by Brown that put Cleveland ahead 33–30 with 48 seconds left. But Jim Bakken kicked his fourth field goal of the day—a 28-yarder—with just five seconds left to tie the score.

September 27—Browns 28, at Philadelphia 20. Cleveland again had to rally to remain unbeaten. This time they trailed 13–7 at halftime after Frank Ryan completed just three of 11 passes. But Ryan threw three touchdowns in the second half. Ross Fichtner returned an interception 64 yards to set up one of those scores.

October 4—Browns 27, Dallas 6. Ryan completed 15 of 26 passes for 256 yards and three touchdowns. "I don't feel I did very well," Ryan said afterward. "I know I can do better." Rookie Paul Warfield had five catches for 123 yards and a touchdown. The victory was a costly one. Defensive tackle Bob Gain fractured his leg, and defensive back Ross Fichtner suffered a concussion.

October 10—Pittsburgh 23, Browns 7. Fullback John Henry Johnson did it all for the Steelers, running for 200 yards and three touchdowns.

Lou Groza missed field-goal attempts of 46 and 45 yards. Ryan threw a 26-yard scoring pass to Collins in the second quarter for the Browns' only score.

October 18—Browns 20, at Dallas 16. Bernie Parrish returned an interception 54 yards for a touchdown to give Cleveland a 20–16 lead with about six and a half minutes left in the Cotton Bowl. The Browns got a break when a touchdown pass from Don Meredith to Tommy McDonald was called back after an official ruled Meredith was beyond the line of scrimmage when he threw the pass. A short time later Meredith fumbled and Jim Kanicki recovered to preserve the victory.

October 25—Browns 42, New York Giants 20. The Giants were their own worst enemies with three interceptions and three fumbles. Rookie halfback Leroy Kelly scored on a 68-yard punt return to give Cleveland a 7–6 lead. Cleveland led 14–13 after three quarters and then scored four more touchdowns in the fourth.

November 1—Browns 30, at Pittsburgh 17. Ernie Green scored two touchdowns in the second half, and Brown ran for 149 yards to become the first player to reach the 10,000-yard career mark (he eventually retired with 10,114 yards). Unlike the first game, Johnson was held to 100 yards in the rematch.

November 8—Browns 34, Washington 24. Brown ran for one touchdown and threw a 13-yard touchdown pass to Collins. Brown finished with 121 yards on 18 carries, while Ryan completed 11 of 19 passes for 162 yards. "Our winning combination today was excellent balance in our offense and defense," Collier said. "Both units played well."

November 15—Browns 37, Detroit 21. Brown ran for 147 yards and two touchdowns, and Walter Beach had two interceptions. He ran the second one back 65 yards for a score. "This was the type of aggressive football we've been wanting," Collier said.

November 22—At Green Bay 28, Browns 21. Cleveland led 14–7 in the third quarter. Green Bay had a fourth-and-one on the Green Bay 44-yard

By the NUMBERS

$8,000—The bonus Gary Collins received for his role as part of the winning team.

$5,000—The value of the Corvette Collins won from *Sport Magazine* for being named the game's Most Valuable Player.

DID YOU KNOW ... That Jim Brown is a man of many talents? In addition to his movie career, in 1964 he wrote a book titled *Off My Chest* and did an off-season column in the *The* (Cleveland) *Plain Dealer* titled "Jim Brown Says."

On May 31, for example, under the headline Cassius and the Black Muslims Not Grave Threat to Country, Brown wrote of the man who would later be known as Muhammad Ali: "We live in a country where a man can worship whatever God he pleases. Although I never could see eye to eye with Cassius' way of worship, I would never criticize his chosen path. And I feel very badly when I see so many slanted articles about Clay and the Muslims."

In a much lighter column on June 7, Brown took exception to *Plain Dealer* sports editor Gordon Cobbledick's comment that golf is not a sport. "I'm not trying to change his mind, but I class it as a sport, and one of the most difficult I've ever tackled. You have to be sharp physically to play it well. It's different from most other sports."

The book proved to be much more controversial than the column. Brown did some television interviews promoting excerpts that were running in *Look* magazine. When he again expressed his tolerance for the Muslims, a bomb threat was called in to one television station and police were called to guard Brown's home.

---

line. With the Browns loading up the line expecting a run, Bart Starr fired a pass to Max McGee, who ran to the Cleveland 1-yard line. Jim Taylor scored from there, and a kick by Paul Hornung tied the score to stun the Browns. "They gambled on that pass, and it paid off for them," Collier said. After a Cleveland fumble, Starr scored on a three-yard bootleg to take control of the game. Green Bay coach Vince Lombardi was gracious in victory. "Cleveland looks like a championship team to me," he said.

November 29—Browns 38, Philadelphia 24. The Browns dominated, taking a 21–3 lead by halftime. Ryan completed 13 of 25 passes for 145 yards and two touchdowns. Brown ran 22 times for 133 yards.

December 6—At St. Louis 28, Browns 19. St. Louis scored 21 points in the second quarter and led 21–6 at halftime. Ryan completed 15 of 33 passes for 242 yards with one touchdown and two interceptions. St. Louis quarterback Charley Johnson completed 15 of 22 passes for 167 yards and two touchdowns as the Cardinals trimmed the Browns lead in the Eastern Division to a half game. "The Cardinals took advantage of their opportunities," Collier said. "We weren't able to make the plays. ... We could not move the ball, and we could not keep the Cardinals from moving it." Modell was undaunted. "We're going to win the title in my old hometown," he predicted.

December 12—Browns 52, at New York Giants 20. Modell was right. Ryan threw five touchdown passes as the Browns crushed the Giants, who had won the title for the past three seasons. "That has to be the greatest game Frank Ryan ever played," said New York coach Allie Sherman. Said Ryan, "Any quarterback can call a helluva game when he gets the help I did out there." A crowd of more than 5,000 met the Browns' plane when it returned to Cleveland.

December 27—Browns 27, Baltimore 0. Collins caught five passes for 130 yards and a championship-game-record three touchdowns and also averaged 44 yards on three punts. Cleveland's defense held Baltimore to 82 yards rushing and 89 yards passing. Johnny Unitas completed 12 of 20 passes with one interception. The Colts also had two fumbles lost. "It was the best defensive game of the year," said Collier, who had signed a new three-year deal the week before the game. "It's the biggest thrill of my career," said Brown, who had 27 carries for 114 yards.

Monday Night Football

Before Howard Cosell pontificated, before Dennis Miller bombed, before Hank Williams Jr. sang, "Are you ready for some football?" *Monday Night Football* was an idea no one was sure would work—a test case for sports, television, and advertising.

In fact, *Monday Night Football* originally was supposed to be *Friday Night Football*. "When word got out we were talking to ABC about *Friday Night Football*, all hell broke out in the congress," former Browns owner Art Modell recalled. "They were trying to protect the high schools and colleges [who play on Friday nights]. We went to congress and got that all straightened out. I appeared before congress as often as some senators," Modell said, chuckling.

The problem was that nobody knew how moving football from a weekend afternoon to prime time on a weeknight would work. According to Modell, ABC had nothing to lose.

"The highest rated program at ABC in those days was a slide that said, 'Technical difficulties. Please stand by,'" Modell joked. "They needed programming, and we needed exposure. It was a sensational gamble for them, but it paid off richly. The ratings are fantastic. There's nothing else that can deliver millions of homes every Monday night with regularity. *Monday Night Football* was one of the great achievements of my professional life."

But no one knew that at the time.

"Anybody who says they thought it would turn into something big is lying," Modell said. "Not a hint. I won't be that daring. I thought it was a good idea, a good experiment."

With his background in television and advertising, Modell was more optimistic about the idea than many of his fellow owners. In fact, when

By the NUMBERS

13-13—The Browns' record for *Monday Night Football*. Individual game results follow:

September 21, 1970—At Cleveland 31, New York Jets 21

December 7, 1970—Cleveland 21, at Houston 10

October 4, 1971—Oakland 34, at Cleveland 20

November 13, 1972—Cleveland 21, at San Diego 17

October 15, 1973—Miami 17, at Cleveland 9

September 26, 1977—At Cleveland 30, New England 27 (OT)

September 24, 1979—At Cleveland 26, Dallas 7

September 15, 1980—Houston 16, at Cleveland 7

November 3, 1980—Cleveland 27, Chicago 21

September 7, 1981—San Diego 44, at Cleveland 14

September 3, 1984—At Seattle 33, Cleveland 0

September 16, 1985—At Cleveland 17, Pittsburgh 7

November 10, 1986—At Cleveland 26, Miami 16

October 26, 1987—At Cleveland 30, L.A. Rams 17

September 19, 1988—At Cleveland 23, Indianapolis 17

November 7, 1988—At Houston 24, Cleveland 17

December 12, 1988—At Miami 38, Cleveland 31

September 25, 1989—At Cincinnati 21, Cleveland 14

October 23, 1989—At Cleveland 27, Chicago 7

October 8, 1990—Cleveland 30, at Denver 29

October 22, 1990—Cincinnati 34, at Cleveland 13

September 14, 1992—Miami 27, at Cleveland 23

September 13, 1993—At Cleveland 23, San Francisco 13

October 2, 1995—Buffalo 22, at Cleveland 19

November 13, 1995—At Pittsburgh 20, Cleveland 3

December 8, 2003—St. Louis 26, at Cleveland 20

TRIVIA

Who were the announcers for ABC's first *Monday Night Football* broadcast?

Answers to the trivia questions are on pages 159–160.

push came to shove, Modell was the only owner to step forward and agree to have his team play in the first *Monday Night Football* game in 1970.

"We were wondering where we should open it up," Modell said. "There was a lot of resistance to it. I had some concerns about it. I was concerned about the steelworker down in Youngstown who'd get home at 1:00 in the morning and get up at 3:00 to go to work. I asked if we could start at 8:00 instead of 9:00, and they wouldn't do it because the West Coast affiliates had to have the 6:00 news. That was sacrosanct.

"So I agreed to take the game, providing I could get the Jets as an opponent. I thought Joe Namath would give us a hell of an audience back east."

For a time, it seemed as if Modell's concerns were valid. "There was a fair advance, but far from a sellout," Modell recalled.

A few hours before game time on September 21, Modell climbed up to the radio booths, located at the top of Cleveland Municipal Stadium. What he saw remained with him for a long, long time.

"The fans came in at the last minute," Modell said. "When we opened up the gates, the general admission buyers came in by the thousands. It was a sight you wouldn't believe—climbing up the hills and down the valleys and across the bridges to buy a ticket to the first Monday night game. It was a sensational opening. It was great. The crowd was enormous and responsive. It was a great thrill."

A standing-room-only, club-record crowd of 85,703 turned out, including National Football League Commissioner Pete Rozelle. An estimated 2,000 fans had to be turned away. The game turned out to be a thriller, as the Browns held off a rally by Namath and the Jets for a 31–21 victory. But neither the next day's papers nor the team's 1970 highlight video made much of the fact that the contest was the first *Monday Night Football* game in history. No one had any idea at the time that it would become a staple of American sporting life and a broadcasting phenomenon—the second-longest-running prime-time show on television after CBS's *60 Minutes*.

Historic or not, it did turn out to be a heck of a game—and quite a debut for the Browns in the American Football Conference. Cleveland took a 14–0 lead in the first quarter. Gary Collins caught an eight-yard pass from quarterback Bill Nelsen to become the first player to score a touchdown on *Monday Night Football*, and then Bo Scott scored on a two-yard run. When Homer Jones returned the second-half kickoff 94 yards for a touchdown, Cleveland took the lead, 21–7. New York's Emerson Boozer scored his second touchdown on a 10-yard run to bring the score to 21–14 before a 27-yard field goal by Don Cockroft pushed the Browns ahead, 24–14, at the end of the third quarter.

But the always brash Namath, who completed 19 of 32 passes for 299 yards, loved the big stage, and he put on quite a show in the fourth

Cleveland defensive ends Jack Gregory (No. 81) and Ron Snidow (No. 88) converge on Jets quarterback Joe Namath in the debut of Monday Night Football.

quarter. It was as if he was trying to reward anybody willing to stay up late enough to watch the end of the game.

After Cockroft missed an 18-yard field goal early in the fourth quarter, Namath drove the Jets 80 yards on four passes, including a 33-yard scoring pass to George Sauer, which brought the score to 24–21 with about three minutes left.

The Browns' offense stalled, and Cleveland had to punt, putting the ball back into Namath's hands on the Jets' 4-yard line with just 1:30 left. A Namath pass moved the ball to the 18, and the quarterback went back to pass again, looking for tight end Pete Lammons. Instead, linebacker Billy Andrews intercepted and ran 25 yards for a touchdown that gave the Browns the first *Monday Night Football* victory.

Even after winning, however, all the Browns praised Namath.

"I'm a Joe Namath fan," Collins told reporters.

"Namath is one of the great all-time passers," Coach Blanton Collier added.

Meanwhile, Namath issued a statement to reporters after the game, saying, "There is nothing I can say after a losing game. Cleveland has a fine football team and we just got beat."

A Rust Belt Rivalry—The Steelers versus the Browns

Nock nock.

Whu's dere?

Sid.

Sid who?

Sid down u dum Browns fans. ΠA. HΛ. HA.

Go Stillers.

That joke, obviously making fun of the intelligence of Pittsburgh Steelers fans, actually appeared on *The* (Cleveland) *Plain Dealer*'s light-hearted Start Page in October 2003, looking ahead to the season-ending game between the Browns and Steelers at Pittsburgh.

In another humorous exercise on the Start Page, a writer created anagrams, scrambling the letters in one word or phrase to make a second word or phrase. Among the phrases: Steelers fans = senses falter. Cowher in playoffs = fawny heroics flop. Iron City = O, cry in it.

To be honest, similar shots are taken at the University of Michigan and its fans every year during the week leading up to the Ohio State–Michigan game. For college football fans in Ohio, that's *the* game. For pro football fans in Cleveland, *the* game comes twice a year—each time the Browns face the Steelers. In fact, the Browns have faced the Steelers more times than any other opponent, and they owned a 55–51 record against their rivals from Pennsylvania through the 2005 season.

Only about 135 miles and a couple of hours on Interstate 76 separate the two cities. A large part of the reason for the rivalry is that the two metropolitan areas are so similar. Each has a rich ethnic and cultural heritage. Originally Rust Belt cities that depended heavily on steel and other manufacturing for their livelihoods, both have enjoyed recent revivals after some hard times. But during those down days, nothing

5—The number of times the Browns and Steelers have gone into overtime while facing each other. The following are the dates and scores of those games:

At Steelers 15, Browns 9, on September 24, 1978

At Steelers 33, Browns 30, on November 25, 1979

At Browns 37, Steelers 31, on November 23, 1986

Steelers 15, at Browns 12, on November 11, 2001

At Steelers 16, Browns 13, on September 29, 2002

made one area feel better than making the other look bad. Sports facilitated that and provided points for comparison. The Browns and the Indians won championships for Cleveland, albeit a long time ago, while the Steelers, the Pirates, and the Penguins have brought championships to Pittsburgh much more recently.

Football, with its rough-and-tumble nature, is a perfect fit for the shot-and-a-beer crowds that populate the many neighborhood taverns in each town. The roots of the sport run deep in those areas. While Ohio produced Paul Brown, Marion Motley, and Bernie Kosar, Pennsylvania has Joe Namath, Mike Ditka, and Dan Marino to its credit. The Steelers' two most successful coaches—Chuck Noll and Bill Cowher—both played for the Browns earlier in their careers.

The teams have taken turns dominating the rivalry, with Cleveland in charge at the start and Pittsburgh in command lately. When the Browns entered the National Football League in 1950 they won the first eight matchups and 16 of the first 18. From 1962 to 1970 the Browns won 14 of the 17 games. When the Steelers were enjoying their greatest success, with Super Bowl victories in 1975, 1976, 1979, and 1980, they went 11–1 against the Browns. In fact, when Three Rivers Stadium opened in 1970, the Browns lost 16 straight games there. From 1984 to

That the Steelers and the Browns have matched up in the playoffs only twice? On January 7, 1995, the Steelers beat the Browns 29–9 at home. The Steelers also bested the Browns 36–33 on January 5, 2003, once again at Pittsburgh.

1989 the Browns went 9–2 overall against the Steelers. But in the 28 meetings since 1990 the Browns have won only seven games.

Of course, there was a break in the action from 1996 to 1998, when the Browns were on hiatus after Art Modell moved his team to Baltimore. That was a trying time for Cleveland fans in more ways than one. While there were some suggestions that they should "adopt" the Steelers as their home team in the interim, die-hard Browns fans really couldn't bring themselves to do that. But cheering for whoever the Steelers were playing each week (or the Baltimore Ravens' opponents, for that matter) didn't quite cut it, either.

It seemed only fitting that the new Browns' first game when they returned to the NFL in 1999 was against the Steelers on ESPN's Sunday night game. But that was before the Steelers spoiled the party with their biggest victory ever over the Browns, 43–0.

Browns wide receiver Quincy Morgan catches this pass against cornerback Deshea Townsend; nonetheless, the Steelers won this wild-card playoff game in January 2003.

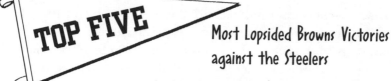

TOP FIVE

Most Lopsided Browns Victories against the Steelers

1. Browns 51, at Steelers 0, on September 10, 1989
2. At Browns 45, Steelers 7, on October 29, 1950
3. At Browns 42, Steelers 7, on December 12, 1954
4. Browns 45, at Steelers 12, October 5, 1958
5. At Browns 41, Steelers 10, on October 8, 1966

Coach Cowher understands the rivalry between the two teams better than almost anyone. He grew up in Pittsburgh and played and coached for the Browns before being named head coach of the Steelers. He used a little deception to fire his team up for that 1999 meeting by telling his players that they were being snubbed by the Browns, who were not going to introduce them during pregame festivities. In reality, Cowher had told Browns officials that he didn't want to intrude on their celebration.

Doug Dieken, former Browns tackle who is now one of the team's broadcasters, played with Cowher during the early 1980s. Dieken admits that he didn't know much about the rivalry when he arrived from the University of Illinois in 1971. But after getting punched in the mouth a couple of times or kneed in the back while unpiling after a play, he caught on quickly. There was a physical nature to the games back then, whether it was "Mean" Joe Greene holding Bob McKay down by his face mask and kicking him in the groin or Joe Jones spiking Terry Bradshaw.

"You've got to go through it to understand it," Dieken said. "Once you get that little extra shove after the whistle, you start to get it. But another factor is the struggles we've had against them. If a championship fight goes to the 10th round before the guy throws the knockout punch, it's a lot more exciting than if the knockout punch is thrown in the first round."

Dieken says the fact that the Browns roster has turned over so many times since the team returned in 1999 plays a factor in diffusing the rivalry, no matter how much the local media or fans try to play it up.

"I look back at the rivalry we had with the Steelers, and we had the same guys for 10 years and so did they," Dieken said. "That's a big part of it. I remember back then we wouldn't even pick up guys who were cut

TOP FIVE

Most Lopsided Steelers Victories against the Browns

1. Steelers 43, at Browns 0, on September 12, 1999
2. Steelers 41, at Browns 0, on December 24, 2005
3. Steelers 42, at Browns 6, on October 5, 1975
4. At Steelers 35, Browns 0, on December 23, 1990
5. At Steelers 30, Browns 0, on December 3, 1972

from the Steelers, no matter how good they were. That has changed. We've got some guys who played for the Steelers, and they've got half our coaching staff."

Dieken remembered approaching former Browns coach Chris Palmer after the Browns won 16–15 at Pittsburgh's Three Rivers Stadium on November 14, 1999, in the rematch of that disappointing opener. Though he was pleased to win, Palmer couldn't understand why Dieken was so excited. "I told him, 'Coach, in the 14 years I played, we never won there,'" Dieken said. "He just didn't know that."

A Boy from Brooklyn Makes Good: Sam Rutigliano

Next to Paul Brown, Sam Rutigliano has to be one of the most popular men ever to coach the Cleveland Browns.

His enthusiasm and outgoing personality, his sense of humor and hilarious one-liners, not to mention his compassion and honesty, were all part of how he became the first man since Brown to coach the Browns without first serving as an assistant with the team.

Players loved him because they knew he cared about them. Fans loved him because of the exciting brand of football he brought with him. Reporters loved him because they never knew what he was going to say, but they knew it wasn't going to be a tired, old cliché.

Need some examples?

Asked about a "critical" stretch in the Browns' season, Rutigliano said, "Critical situations are in war and surgery."

Asked about the possibility of a jinx when the Browns lost for the 12th time in as many visits to Pittsburgh's Three Rivers Stadium, he said, "Save it for Halloween. Get a costume and go trick or treat. There is no such thing [as a jinx], just good football teams who play well. It's a naïve question. It deserves a naïve answer."

He was a natural for the television career that followed after he was fired by the Browns in 1984. Even after returning to coaching at Liberty University for 11 seasons, he retired and took another television job in Cleveland; he had never sold his home in Waite Hill.

"When we came back [to Cleveland] after we beat Cincinnati in the regular-season finale in 1980, at that time in this town, I realized whatever else I did when I left the Browns, I was going to stay," Rutigliano said. "That team really, truly identified with this city's unbelievable love affair with the Browns."

His sense of humor remains intact.

In talking about today's National Football League players, he said, "Too much attitude, and not enough gratitude. ... Everybody's got a dollar sign where the soul was."

Asked about playing golf (or, as the case may be, not playing it) in retirement, he said, "I grew up in New York City. First time I saw a golf course, I thought it was a cemetery."

Rutigliano grew up in Brooklyn, where his father, Joe, lived after leaving Bari, Italy, with his parents when he was 10 years old. Joe Rutigliano drove a truck for Ebinger's Bakery, and his wife, Mary, worked in the bakery. They had three sons, with Sam in the middle. The family lived in a two-bedroom apartment.

Sam became a star playing wide receiver at Erasmus Hall High School and was recruited by the University of Tennessee, a fact that delighted his father even if he didn't quite believe someone was going to pay for his son's education in return for services on the football field. But the high school coaches went on strike during Sam's senior year, and, without sports to keep him going, Rutigliano dropped out of high school and got a job delivering telegrams. Tennessee arranged for him to attend Eastern Central Junior College in Decatur, Mississippi, and he eventually earned his high school diploma from Newton County Agricultural School, a fact that delighted city slicker Sam Rutigliano to no end.

When he finally got to Tennessee in 1951, Rutigliano was forced to sit out his freshman year because he'd attended a junior college. He could only watch as Tennessee went undefeated and won the national championship under Coach Robert R. Neyland. Neyland retired before the next season and was replaced by Harvey Robinson, who told Rutigliano—who was splitting time between receiver and defensive end—that he wouldn't make the traveling squad as a sophomore.

Disappointed by how he was being treated, Rutigliano quit school and moved home, eventually transferring to the University of Tulsa for his final two years. He realized his playing career was over, so after getting his bachelor of arts degree from Tulsa, he got his

TRIVIA

What former American Football League Coach of the Year gave Sam Rutigliano his first job in pro football?

Answers to the trivia questions are on pages 159–160.

Sam Rutigliano always had something interesting to say as coach of the Browns.
Photo courtesy of Bettmann/CORBIS.

master's degree in education from Columbia University and pursued his goal of becoming a high school teacher and coach.

From 1956 to 1964 Rutigliano coached at Lafayette High School in Brooklyn, Horace Greeley High School in Chappaqua, New York, and Greenwich High School in Greenwich, Connecticut. Then it was on to college coaching as an assistant at Connecticut and Maryland before spending 11 years as an NFL assistant with Denver, New England, the New York Jets, and the New Orleans Saints. Then finally Art Modell made him the sixth head coach of the Browns on Christmas Eve in 1977.

Much had happened since the Browns won the NFL championship under Blanton Collier in 1964. They had lost the NFL title to the Green Bay Packers 23–12 after the 1965 season. They lost to the Baltimore Colts 34–0 in the NFL championship game in 1968. They lost to the Minnesota Vikings 27–7 after the 1969 season. Collier went 7–7 in 1970 and was replaced by Nick Skorich in 1971. Skorich led the team to the playoffs during his first two seasons, but after going 7–5–2 in 1973 and 4–10 in

1974, he was replaced by Forrest Gregg. Gregg failed to make the playoffs in any of his three seasons and was replaced by former Browns player Dick Modzelewski for the last game of the 1977 season as the Browns finished 6–8.

Enter Rutigliano.

"He was a breath of fresh air," guard Robert E. Jackson said of Rutigliano. "He came in and pretty much let us go to a wide-open offense. He had all those quirky quotes, but he really cared for the players."

Rutigliano went 8–8 in 1978 and 9–7 in 1979 before quarterback Brian Sipe and the Kardiac Kids, known for their close games and late rallies, raced to a heart-stopping 11–5 in 1980, a promising season that ended prematurely on the infamous "Red Right 88" end-zone interception on the final play of a playoff game against the Oakland Raiders.

Rutigliano went 5–11 in 1981, 4–5 in the strike-shortened 1982 season, and 9–7 in 1983. But when the 1984 team lost seven of its first eight games, Modell fired Rutigliano on October 21, 1984.

As any coach would, Rutigliano had some regrets and wished he would have done some things differently. One of those regrets involved Tom Cousineau. Cousineau was a standout linebacker at St. Edward High School in Lakewood and then at Ohio State University. He was the number one pick in the 1979 draft, taken by the Buffalo Bills. But negotiations with the Bills got off to a bad start, and he wound up playing with Montreal in the Canadian Football League. Eventually the Bills traded him to the Browns in 1982. Despite playing well, Cousineau fell out of favor with defensive coordinator Marty Schottenheimer, and when Schottenheimer took over for the fired Rutigliano, Cousineau's days were numbered. He finished his career with the San Francisco 49ers.

"Tom Cousineau was on my watch," Rutigliano said. "Tom Cousineau was an outstanding player. Frankly, I don't think Marty Schottenheimer felt he was. I totally disagree. I think Tom Cousineau was handled very, very poorly, because I think he could have been a

That Sam Rutigliano grew up in the Sheepshead Bay section of Brooklyn, the same neighborhood that produced Vince Lombardi and Joe Paterno?

By the NUMBERS

Sam Rutigliano was one of the most popular coaches in Browns history, and his teams were among the most beloved. In 1980 attendance reached 620,496, still a single-season high for the team. Attendance by years under Rutigliano:

510,046—1978

593,821—1979

620,496—1980

601,725—1981

251,314—1982 (A strike reduced the home season to four games.)

564,639—1983

458,433—1984

great player. I brought him in. I coached him. And I think it was a big mistake pushing him out."

Conversely, if there was one thing Rutigliano was most proud of during his time with the Browns, it was the development of the Inner Circle program, which helps players struggling with drug or alcohol addictions. "It's unbelievable what those guys have done with themselves," said Rutigliano, who still abides by the promise to keep the identities of those who participate in the program a secret. "It not only prolonged their careers, but it saved their lives."

After leaving the Browns, Rutigliano rejected all offers to return to the NFL. "I was in my early fifties," he explained. "I wanted to prove I could do something else. I got into television. I enjoyed that. You got paid and you didn't have to win."

In 1988 he wrote his autobiography, *Pressure*, which included touching descriptions of how he met and wooed his wife, Barb, and how they suffered through the loss of one daughter, who was killed in a car crash when she was four and a half years old, and the suicide attempt of another.

In the course of promoting the book Rutigliano spoke to a group of televangelists, including Reverend Jerry Falwell. Falwell invited the former coach to speak at the chapel at his school, Liberty University, and eventually offered Rutigliano the head football coach job.

"I knew I needed to coach again," Rutigliano said. "My wife said, 'You always said you'd like to go to a small Christian school and coach.' A lot of people talk about wanting to have God's will determine where you go and what you do. I thought to myself, 'He ain't gonna send me a Federal Express.'

"It was a great experience. When you go to Liberty, you have to take a vow of poverty. Jerry takes the vow and you take the poverty."

Rutigliano coached there from 1989 to 1999 and went 67–53, including 9–2 in 1997. He retired in 2000 at the age of 67—for about an hour—before accepting a job with NFL Europe, and he has since spent six years in Barcelona, Scotland, and Hamburg.

A Champion at Any Age: Brian Sipe

Sam Rutigliano admitted he was surprised when he heard that former Browns quarterback Brian Sipe was going to become football coach at Santa Fe Christian High School in Solana Beach, California.

After all, it had taken Sipe a few seasons on the Browns' taxi squad before he figured out he really wanted to be a pro football player. Even then, the well-rounded Sipe had so many other interests that it seemed his future after football would lead him to work with music, politics, history, geography, travel, literature, or architecture.

As a matter of fact, he was designing custom homes when officials at Santa Fe Christian persuaded him to take over their football program in 2001 after he helped coach the school's quarterbacks for a year.

"I had so much fun working with the kids and smelling the grass again," Sipe told *The San Diego Union-Tribune*. "I rediscovered football. ... If six months ago you would have told me I'd take this job, I'd have said you were crazy. But I've always loved high school football. It's the game in its purest form."

Sipe instituted a tough conditioning program during the summer as well as team dinners and bible studies during the season. He has taken his team backpacking to build camaraderie. All that he has done has worked, as Santa Fe Christian has won three of the past five small-school titles in California.

"I don't want to sound heroic," he told the *Akron Beacon Journal*. "I can be part of something going on in my community. I can be of some help. I've got the time, and I don't want to miss the opportunity."

Rutigliano wasn't surprised at all by the way Sipe felt about coaching. "One of the things that's interesting about coaching is that everybody sees it as guys wanting to win, but I think it's more than that,"

By the NUMBERS

Browns Records Still Held by Brian Sipe

23,713—Career passing yards

4,132—Passing yards in a single season

3,439—Career passes attempted

1,944—Career passes completed

567—Passes attempted in a single season

444—Passing yards in one game

337—Completions in a single season

154—Career touchdown passes

57—Passes attempted in one game

30—Passing touchdowns in a single season

18—Most 300-yard games in a career

said the former Browns coach. "I think he [Sipe] really felt like he made a contribution. I think he felt the joy and how much you get back when you go into a profession like that. Having been a high school coach, the best relationships I have now are with the guys I coached in high school. It's just a different experience. There's so much more to it.

"I was surprised he went into it, but I was not surprised at the reward he would get from it."

Football has been only one part of Sipe's life. True to his California roots, he learned to surf as an eighth grader. By that time he had already experienced success as an athlete, having played catcher and center field as an 11-year-old on the Northern El Cajon/La Mesa Little League team that won the Little League World Series in 1961. He called that experience the thrill of a lifetime. The trip to Williamsport, Pennsylvania, was the first time he'd been on an airplane. The icing on the cake was being featured in a celebration photograph that ran in *Life* magazine.

As he told *The San Diego Union-Tribune*, that experience has stayed with him throughout his athletic career. "I think I'm one of the very few who played on a [Little League] championship team who went on to have a professional career in sports," said Sipe, who was inducted into the Little League Hall of Fame. "I can't forget that Williamsport was a formative experience for me, one that helped me

Quarterback Brian Sipe still holds many Browns records. Photo courtesy of Diamond Images.

during my professional football career. The coaches kept us focused. I don't think we comprehended the bigness of it until it was over. That's when the euphoria set in."

He became co–California Interscholastic Federation Player of the Year as a quarterback at Grossmont High School before setting numerous records for pass-happy Don Coryell at San Diego State. No wonder he caught the eye of Browns scouts. Cleveland was still in the market for a quarterback after stunning their fans by trading star receiver Paul Warfield to Miami in exchange for the third pick in the 1970 draft, which they used to acquire Purdue's Mike Phipps.

That move didn't pay off the way the Browns had hoped it would, so in 1972 they took Sipe, the 1971 NCAA passing champion, in the 13th round. In 1974, after the Browns lost five of their first six games, Sipe replaced Phipps in the fourth quarter in a game against Denver on October 27 at Cleveland Municipal Stadium. With Cleveland trailing 21–9, Sipe scored two touchdowns in the last six minutes for a 23–21 victory. He became the full-time starter in 1976. Phipps was traded to the Bears in 1978.

Sipe became a fan favorite, leading the team through some of its most thrilling times—and one of its most heartbreaking. He was, after all, the quarterback who threw the infamous last-minute interception in the AFC divisional playoff game against Oakland on the play known as Red Right 88 on January 4, 1981. It wasn't the ending anyone had in mind when Sipe was named the most valuable player in the NFL In 1980, when he completed 337 of 554 passes for 4,132 yards and 30 touchdowns while leading the Kardiac Kids to the AFC Central title past defending Super Bowl champion Pittsburgh.

"I've never been around a guy who did so much with his God-given talents," Rutigliano said. "He was not a prototype guy like Terry Bradshaw or John Elway or Dan Marino. He was a real, genuine guy who was never affected by all the great things that happened to him."

Sipe stayed on as the Browns' quarterback for three more seasons before signing a three-year, $2-million deal with the New Jersey Generals in the short-lived USFL in 1983. He finished his playing career with Jacksonville in 1985.

TRIVIA

Before attending San Diego State, what college did Brian Sipe attend?

Answers to the trivia questions are on pages 159–160.

Tough Choices Pay Off for Ozzie Newsome

When he was going into sixth grade, Ozzie Newsome made a decision that would impact the rest of his life. He decided to transfer from the school he'd been attending, Leighton Training, to Leighton Elementary, where he would be the only African American in his class.

"It broadened my horizons," Newsome said. "It taught me humility. It taught me how to deal with other people and taught them how to deal with me.

"It was a challenge early on, but when you're dealing with 11- and 12-year-olds, they tend to accept you for what you are and not what's being said at home."

It turned out to be the right decision for Newsome. It also set a precedent. When faced with a tough choice, Newsome tends to make the right decisions about his future.

He decided to concentrate on football instead of baseball. He decided to attend Alabama instead of Auburn. And when Art Modell moved his football team to Baltimore after the 1995 season, Newsome, the Browns' all-time leading receiver, decided to go with him.

"The decision to come wasn't difficult," said Newsome, who retired in 1990 and worked as a scout, a coach, and then in the player personnel department with the Browns before joining the Ravens and becoming the first African American general manager in the NFL. "If I wanted to stay in professional football, I had to make the move. Plus, I was getting promoted to being head of football operations. The opportunity was there. It was something I had worked for. So the decision to make the move wasn't that bad. Living with the decision—continuing to live in Cleveland and then to move a family from one city to the next—that was not an easy thing to do."

TOP TEN

The Browns' Top 10 Career Receivers

1.	662	Ozzie Newsome
2.	331	Gary Collins
3.	323	Greg Pruitt
4.	315†	Brian Brennan
	315†	Kevin Johnson
6.	310	Reggie Rucker
7.	305	Webster Slaughter
8.	297	Eric Metcalf
9.	281	Ray Renfro
10.	276	Earnest Byner

Like many of the employees who made the move, Newsome was called a traitor and received hate mail. When he was elected to the Pro Football Hall of Fame in 1999, on the eve of the Browns' return, he was worried about appearing in Canton. But the worry dissolved after he received a rousing reception from the fans, complete with barking and the chanting of his name.

"I did not know what that reception was going to be," he admitted. "In the end, you find out that people really appreciated what I did as a player. A Browns fan is a Browns fan. They really came out and supported me. That was unbelievable."

Newsome was born on March 16, 1956, in Muscle Shoals, Alabama, a rural town in the northwest corner of the state about 120 miles north of Birmingham. His father owned a restaurant called Fats Cafe. His mother was a housekeeper. One of five children, Newsome picked cotton and mowed lawns as a kid, but it was his work in the classroom and as an athlete that got him noticed and eased that transition into the previously all-white Leighton Elementary School.

He was a catcher on the baseball team and started as a point guard on the basketball team before a growth spurt left him as the tallest player on the squad. He excelled at those sports before emerging as a football player in high school. He played linebacker, safety, and wide receiver for the Colbert County High School football team, which lost only three games in the three years Newsome was a starter.

That team won a state title when Newsome was a junior, and he thought about joining quarterback Phil Gargis at Auburn, where he wouldn't have to compete for playing time with former high school teammate Thad Flanagan, who attended Alabama. In the end, however, he decided on Alabama, becoming the first freshman football player to start at the school. Nicknamed "The Wizard of Oz" by venerable coach Bear Bryant, Newsome would finish with 102 receptions for 2,070 yards and became one of the most popular players in the history of the program.

Newsome credits Bryant with teaching him how to catch a ball. "He taught me to look it all the way in," Newsome said. "People don't realize that the ball is not completely caught until it's tucked away. Every time I would make a catch, if I didn't completely tuck the ball in, he would comment from his tower."

He learned other lessons from Bryant as well. "He talked about having your own initiative," Newsome said. "He talked about wanting to overachieve for yourself, the importance of teamwork, the importance of being held accountable. Those are some of the lessons he taught. You can see how important they are even today."

When the NFL draft rolled around, four or five teams were interested in Newsome; some of them, including the Browns, wanted him to switch from wide receiver to tight end. Browns coach Sam Rutigliano told him, "You can be a good wide receiver or you can be a great tight end."

The position didn't matter to Newsome. "The only thing that made a difference to me was that they said they were going to throw me the ball," he said. "That's what I hung my hat on. They said they were not going to just make me a blocker. They said they were going to utilize my skills and throw me the football, and they did."

In 13 seasons with the Browns, from 1978 to 1990, he caught more passes than any other receiver in team history—662 for 7,980 yards and 47 touchdowns. His dependability was legendary. He rarely dropped a ball. He did not fumble in his last 557 catches or carries, and he played in 198 straight games.

TRIVIA

Alabama wide receiver Ozzie Newsome was one of two first-round draft choices for the Browns in 1978. Who was the other?

Answers to the trivia questions are on pages 159–160.

Ozzie Newsome heads for the end zone with his 500ᵗʰ career reception in this 1985 game against the Oilers.

Rutigliano called Newsome the most talented player he coached—and one of the most likable. "I don't know anybody I've ever been around who didn't like Ozzie Newsome," Rutigliano said.

Most of Newsome's memories of the Browns are good ones, and he's learned to live with the ones that aren't so good—like The Drive and The Fumble in the AFC Championship games after the 1986 and 1987 seasons, respectively. "You use them as building blocks," Newsome said. "The Drive and The Fumble prevented me from actually playing in the Super Bowl. You still have that emptiness. But you learn how to deal with disappointment and how to take that disappointment and make yourself a better person."

After his retirement, Modell hired Newsome as a special assignment scout. Two years later Newsome became assistant to the head coach/offense/pro personnel. About that time he decided he liked the player personnel side of the football operation more than the coaching side.

"Coaching was great," he said. "I enjoyed the interaction with the players. But the evaluation of players, I just enjoyed that more. There's a little more instant gratification in coaching. In personnel, it takes sometimes two or three years."

It has been 10 years since Newsome moved to Baltimore, 16 years since he retired as a player. The ties to both Cleveland and Baltimore remain strong.

"I work for Baltimore," Newsome said. "I put all my energy into this. I'm a Baltimore Raven. But I only played for two teams—Alabama and the Cleveland Browns. Cleveland's always going to be a special place for me."

The Kardiac Kids

It has been 26 years since the Kardiac Kids won the hearts of Browns fans—26 years since their thrilling exploits gave a downtrodden city something to cheer for.

After the river caught fire, after the city declared bankruptcy, after Ten Cent Beer Night caused a riot at Cleveland Municipal Stadium that made the Indians the laughingstock of the country, somebody had to do something to restore civic pride.

That somebody turned out to be the Browns' Kardiac Kids.

"There was a love affair between the city and the players," said guard Robert E. Jackson. "I don't know if you could duplicate that. It was unique."

Even now, 26 years later, fans around the world still approach Coach Sam Rutigliano and want to shake his hand.

"They say thanks for the memories or that was the greatest time or that was the most fun," said Rutigliano, who still lives in the Cleveland area and works on a Browns show for WKYC TV. "Almost all their stories start the same way: 'My father...'

"I think in a lot of places they would have gone on to other things. But not in Cleveland."

A newspaper writer came up with the nickname, and nothing could have been more accurate. Although "Kardiac Kids" usually refers to the 1980 Browns and their penchant for routinely snatching victory from the jaws of defeat, the trend actually started during the 1979 season, when 12 of 16 games were decided by seven points or less. That team finished 9–7 and missed the playoffs.

The start of the 1980 season gave no indication of the great things that were in store. The Browns lost their opener at New England, 34–17,

Quarterback Brian Sipe (No. 17) was the heart of the Kardiac Kids. Photo courtesy of Getty Images.

and their home opener to Houston, 16–7, on *Monday Night Football.* Then came a 20–13 victory over Kansas City and a 34–27 escape at Tampa Bay with the Buccaneers driving to the Browns' 20 as time expired. The Browns lost 19–16 to Denver, and then they won 27–3 at Seattle.

But the next four games—all victories—started hearts pounding all over northeast Ohio. Quarterback Brian Sipe threw a 46-yard touchdown pass to Dave Logan with 16 seconds left to beat the Green Bay Packers 26–21. Pittsburgh, playing without Terry Bradshaw, Lynn Swann, John

Stallworth, Franco Harris, and Jack Lambert, still built a 26–14 lead, which Sipe then erased with two late touchdown passes for a 27–26 victory. The Browns beat the Chicago Bears 27–21 and squeaked by at Baltimore 28–27, although they had to recover onside kicks in the final minutes of both games to hold on.

They lost 16–13 at Pittsburgh and crushed Cincinnati 31–7 before finishing the season with another heart-stopping flurry. They took a one-game lead in the American Football Conference's Central Division with a 17–14 victory at Houston, preserved by Clarence Scott's interception with 1:17 left. They wasted a 10–0 lead against the New York Jets, needing a fourth-quarter touchdown pass from Sipe to Greg Pruitt for a 17–14 victory. They lost 28–23 at Minnesota on a 46-yard Hail Mary pass from Tommy Kramer to Ahmad Rashad as time expired. They won their first AFC Central Division title since 1971 with a 27–24 victory at Cincinnati, a victory achieved with a 22-yard field goal by Don Cockroft with 1:25 left and then a game-saving tackle by Ron Bolton, who stopped wide receiver Steve Kreider inbounds on the Browns' 14, allowing the clock to run out. The Browns had made the playoffs for the first time since 1972.

Pure pandemonium ensued—on the field and back in Cleveland, where thousands of fans packed into the airport to welcome home the team, which again had 12 of 16 games decided by seven points or less.

"There were so many people in the airport, they had the buses meet us at the plane, because we couldn't walk through the airport," Jackson recalled. "They set up a stage for us near the IX Center, and we each walked across the platform. The mayor was there. There were thousands

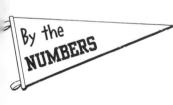

Quarterback Brian Sipe in 1980

4,132—yards*

554—attempts

337—completions*

91.37—rating

30—touchdowns*

14—interceptions

*Team single-season record

Starting Lineup

The Starting Lineup for the 1980 Browns (the Kardiac Kids)

Offense

WR	Dave Logan
LT	Doug Dieken
LG	Henry Sheppard
C	Tom DeLeone
RG	Joe DeLamielleure
RT	Cody Risien
TE	Ozzie Newsome
WR	Reggie Rucker
QB	Brian Sipe
FB	Mike Pruitt
RB	Greg Pruitt

Defense

LDE	Marshall Harris
NT	Henry Bradley
RDE	Lyle Alzado
LOLB	Charlie Hall
LILB	Robert L. Jackson
RILB	Dick Ambrose
ROLB	Clay Matthews
LCB	Ron Bolton
RCB	Clinton Burrell
FS	Thom Darden
SS	Clarence Scott

of people everywhere. They were climbing over fences and standing on cars."

According to Jackson, the reason that team was so successful was because of the chemistry among the players, a bond that remained in force when more than 20 players returned to celebrate the 25th anniversary of the Kardiac Kids in March 2005. "We were a very close-knit group," Jackson said. "That made it special."

As it so often does, the closeness started on the offensive line. Interestingly, that was the year guard Joe DeLamielleure joined the Browns after the preseason. Tackle Doug Dieken was in contract talks with the Browns, and the negotiations were not going well. So on the Monday after the last preseason game, Dieken drove home to Streator, Illinois. The players were off on Tuesday. But while they were away, the Browns traded for DeLamielleure and then came to terms with Dieken, who drove back before reporters even realized he was gone. When DeLamielleure joined the mix, he rotated at guard with Robert E. (Bob) Jackson and Henry Sheppard.

"Our job was to pass protect for Brian Sipe, and we were as good as there was in the NFL at pass protection," Jackson said. "If they brought five guys, we picked those guys up. We always had the maximum number of receivers out on every pattern for Brian.

"Brian exuded confidence. We believed we were never out of a game. Brian was a great leader and set the tone for us."

Jackson said that while Sipe was blessed with charisma, fans didn't realize how tough he was. "These were the days before the documenting of concussions," Jackson said. "Brian Sipe suffered so many concussions it was scary. It got to the point where guys would just look at him and he got a concussion. So we knew that even if it meant getting a holding penalty, we were not going to let them touch him. We'd always tell him to put his mouthpiece in. Sometimes we'd be in the huddle and I don't think he knew where he was. Sometimes it took a group effort to get him through. But he never complained."

After that season Rutigliano was named Coach of the Year in the NFL and Sipe was named the Most Valuable Player in the NFL, the last Brown so honored.

Kardiac Arrest

Red Right 88.

Those words send chills up and down the spines of true Browns fans.

Cleveland was used to championship football during the Browns' early years. The team played for a league title during all of its first 10 seasons in existence—four in the All-America Football Conference and six in the National Football League.

But times changed after the Browns won their last National Football League championship in 1964. They lost the title games in 1965, 1968, and 1969, and they failed to even make the playoffs from 1973 to 1979. Then came 1980 and the thrilling bunch of players nicknamed the Kardiac Kids. Unheralded in the preseason and 0–2 after the first two weeks of play, quarterback Brian Sipe, the Most Valuable Player in the NFL that season, rallied the troops and led the Browns to an 11–5 record in the regular season. Browns fans dared to hope another championship was within their grasp.

They clung to that hope until the final minutes of a game against the Oakland Raiders on January 4, 1981, a frigid day in Cleveland Municipal Stadium. Sipe drove the Browns 73 yards in the closing minutes. But on a second-and-nine from the Oakland 13, a Sipe pass intended for Ozzie Newsome was intercepted by Raiders safety Mike Davis in the end zone with 41 seconds left. Oakland had earned a 14–12 victory in the AFC divisional playoff.

The front page of *The Plain Dealer* the next day showed a picture of an anguished Sipe holding his head in his right hand as if to say, "What have I done?" The headline read "Kardiac Kids Run Out of Miracles."

If the front page of the paper offered a fairly straightforward look at the outcome of the game, the sports pages offered more of an analytical take. "Kardiac Arrest," read one headline, followed by, "Browns' Season Ends on Questionable Call of 'Red Right 88' Pass." An opinion piece by Hal Lebovitz ran under the headline: "Pass? Browns Had to Try Field Goal." Underneath those stories was a picture of Raiders players celebrating while a dejected Newsome sat frozen at their feet on the ground.

Lebovitz called Coach Sam Rutigliano to task:

I'm going to give Sam Rutigliano the benefit of the doubt. He must have thought Don Cockroft couldn't kick a field goal in the open end of the stadium. But I don't consider that a valid reason.

For me, he *had* to give Cockroft that opportunity. Not even if someone had a gun at my back would I have put the ball in the

This interception by Mike Davis (No. 36) left Ozzie Newsome (No. 82), the Browns, and their fans out in the cold during the 1981 AFC playoff game.

6—Number of categories in which the Browns outdid the Raiders in the 1980 AFC divisional playoff game. Not that it matters—despite owning the statistical edge, the Browns lost the game.

	Cleveland	**Los Angeles**
First Downs	17	12
Net Yards	254	208
Net Yards Rushing	85	76
Net Yards Passing	169	132
Net Punt Average	39.3	29.3
Penalties/Yards Lost	2/10	5/39
Time of Possession	27:27	32:33

air when the Browns were on the 13-yard line, 56 seconds to go and a field goal would have won it. ...

But if someone had a gun at Sam's back, he'd play Russian roulette and hope one chamber was empty, living dangerously as always. That's his style, so he'll never know if Cockroft could have made that short one or not.

In fact, Cockroft had missed field-goal attempts of 47 and 30 yards as well as an extra point after a bad snap. That left the Browns with a 6–0 lead after a 42-yard interception return by Ron Bolton midway through the second quarter. Mark Van Eeghen scored on a one-yard run with 18 seconds left in the second quarter to put Oakland in front 7–6 at half-time. Cockroft hit field goals of 30 and 29 yards in the third quarter as the Browns took a 12–7 lead, but another one-yard run by Van Eeghen with 5:38 left gave Oakland a 14–12 lead and set the stage for heartbreak.

The ill-fated play was called by Rutigliano and quarterback coach Jim Shofner.

"We felt a field goal was no gut cinch," Rutigliano told reporters after the game. "It was our plan to throw on second down, then run the ball on third down, and if we didn't get it into the end zone by then, go for the field goal. The play we called was a play that has been successful in the past. Unfortunately, it was an errant throw. But I'd rather put my money on Sipe's arm than take a chance on a field-goal attempt. But the fact also is if we had made the field goals earlier in the game, it would not have gotten to what it did at the end."

Sipe admitted he questioned the play call at first, then relented.

"I thought we would run the ball and in so doing set up a field goal," Sipe told reporters after the game. "Running the ball seemed to be the logical thing to do, but the staff was adamant. I listened to them because they are smart, they know what they are doing, and also, that play has worked often for us the last two years."

Sipe's original target was Dave Logan, but when Sipe saw Oakland free safety Burgess Owens coming up, he looked for Newsome.

"I was behind Davis and then Burgess Owens came back to me and forced me to take a couple of steps up field," Newsome told reporters after the game. "When I saw the ball coming and felt Davis against my arm, I knew I was in trouble. I tried to knock the ball away from him, but I couldn't reach it. It was a good call, a great call; give Davis and Owens credit for beating it. We lived and died with the pass all year, and this time we died by it."

Sipe took the blame for a bad throw.

"It was not the play; it was the execution that was bad," he told reporters.

Said Davis to reporters, "I was surprised he threw in that situation. Sipe had to get rid of it, working against the clock and all. But man, I don't think anyone could have completed that pass. ... Yeah, that was the biggest play in my career."

What made things even worse?

"I was open," Logan told reporters that day. "If Brian had stayed on me longer, he would have realized it."

That *Plain Dealer* sportswriter Chuck Heaton, one of the reporters who covered the Browns' shocking loss on January 4, 1981, is the father of Emmy-winning actress Patricia Heaton of television's *Everybody Loves Raymond*? In that show the character of her husband, portrayed by actor Ray Romano, is a sportswriter.

Players and fans who were there that day remember the absolute quiet that descended on the stadium after that terrible play, as if the temperature (1°) with windchills ranging from minus 18° to minus 36° actually froze all those present. Somehow the dazed Browns made their way to the locker room, which was equally silent.

Sipe and Rutigliano valiantly tried to keep things in perspective.

"Yes, I have feelings of regret and despair about losing this game, but fused with them is the knowledge that we had a good year," Sipe told reporters. "I think we lifted the feelings of everybody around here, and I don't want to hear anybody bad rap us. And I don't just mean me. I mean everybody. ... It was a good year, even if it ended too soon."

Asked if the loss was his toughest in 26 years of coaching, Rutigliano told reporters, "There is no toughest thing. The only thing that's tough is death."

The Dawg Pound

There is some controversy about how the infamous Dawg Pound actually got its name.

Cornerbacks Hanford Dixon and Frank Minnifield are often credited with the concept, and there is no doubt they raised the profile of that east section of the stadium to the unprecedented heights it enjoys to this day. They're as well known for that as they are for the talent and pregame preparation that made them one of the best defensive back tandems in both team and league history.

But some Browns insiders claim that the original idea for the Dawg Pound's name came from the late Eddie Johnson, a tough linebacker and a Georgia native. Although Johnson attended the University of Louisville, the University of Georgia's nickname is the Bulldogs. "How 'bout them Dawgs?" is a popular catchphrase in Johnson's home state.

At any rate, the Dawg Pound made a name for itself starting in the 1980s, when rowdy fans barked their support, often throwing dog biscuits, bones, and who knows what else at opposing players. More than once officials had to move play to the other end of the field in order to escape the fever pitch in the Pound.

This was no faceless mob, either. The characters had names and personalities. John "Big Dawg" Thompson wore a bloodhound mask and an orange construction helmet with brown and white stripes down the middle. Vince "D-Dawg" Erwin had a television gig during one season. The "Bone Lady," with her dangling bone jewelry, was featured in a 2005 McDonald's commercial with rookies Charlie Frye and Braylon Edwards.

Based solely on appearances, Geoff Morton is an unlikely denizen of the Dawg Pound. Tall and stately with a shock of white hair and dark-rimmed glasses, he appears more suited to his day job—director of

A Dawg-day afternoon in Cleveland.

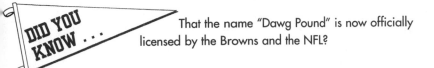

college counseling for St. Edward High School, a boys Catholic prep school run by the Brothers of Holy Cross in the Cleveland suburb of Lakewood. As a 13-year-old boy, Morton paid 25¢ to sit in the bleachers and watch the Browns beat the Los Angeles Rams, 30–28, for their first NFL Championship in their first season, 1950, in the NFL.

"We were right there, smack up against the field," Morton said. "They were the best seats in the stadium. My two brothers and I had gone downtown by ourselves. After the game we leaped out of the bleachers and onto the field. Nobody tried to chase us away. The players stayed on the field to shake hands."

So for the better part of 50 years, on any Sunday the Browns were at home, Morton, a former basketball and tennis coach, sat with an assortment of family and friends smack dab in the middle of the Dawg Pound. Although never the face-paint, dog-ears, or bare-beer-belly type, he took it all in and loved every minute of it.

"I think it's a great seat," he said. "I love sitting there. I wouldn't sit anywhere else."

A friend from Detroit once invited Morton to sit in the owner's loge. "I hated it," Morton said. "It just wasn't the same atmosphere. These are the real fans. In the old days people would pass around food, buckets of chicken, even joints. When it rained, everybody put up these big tarps and spread them over everybody else."

Somebody once gave his wife a ticket worth $250. "By halftime she was back in the Dawg Pound," Morton said. "She said no one was cheering up there."

Morton has seen some amazing things from his vantage point in the Pound.

For instance, before nets were installed to catch field goals and extra points, there was a free-for-all anytime a kick went into the stands, Morton recalled. "They tried different things," he said. "First of all, whoever caught it got to keep it. Of course, there were a lot of fights. Then they announced the police would put it away and keep it safe for

By the NUMBERS

Browns' Browns

20—Number of players named Brown who played for the Browns. They were the following:

Bobby Brown, WR, 2000, 2001*

Courtney Brown, DE, 2000–04

Dante Brown, RB, 2004*

Dean Brown, DB, 1969

Dee Brown, RB, 2004

Eddie Brown, DB, 1974–75

James Brown, OL, 2000

Jerome Brown, DL, 1993*

Jim Brown, RB, 1957–65

John Brown, T, 1962–66

John Brown III, WR, 1992*

Ken Brown, RB, 1970–75

Lomas Brown, T, 1999

Marvin Brown, FB, 2002*

Orlando Brown, T 1994–95, 1999

Preston Brown, KR, 1984

Richard Brown, LB, 1991–92

Stan Brown, WR, 1971

Terry Brown, DB, 1976

Thomas Brown, DE, 1981, 1983

*On practice squad, but did not play in a game.

whoever caught it. Then they were going to donate the balls to charity. Of course, then people started to play keep-away with them. I saw one guy pull out a knife and deflate one."

After the 2005 season, Morton sadly reported:

It used to be a lot rowdier.

I remember one Sunday a guy showed up in a pink linen jacket, a yellow shirt, and a paisley tie. Well, it wasn't long before somebody threw a beer on the guy and there was a big fight.

Another time I remember some huge Steelers fan beating up a Browns fan. The guy sitting next to me took out a blackjack and hit him over the head with it. Then he turned to me and said, "He was blocking my view." It wasn't that he was defending the Browns fan. The Steelers fan was in his way.

Another time Morton treated a student to a game. The boy had a very short crew cut, and somebody threw a dog biscuit that glanced off the boy's head, opening a gash in his scalp that bled profusely. "We had to take him out of there," said Morton, whose enthusiasm for the area was not dampened by the incident.

One of the most memorable moments for Morton was the day the Browns introduced Ernie Davis to the crowd before an exhibition game in 1962. Davis, a first-round draft choice obtained by the Browns in a trade, had contracted leukemia and would be dead in a year. Rumors of his condition circulated, although it had not been officially reported by the media. He was wearing street clothes when he was introduced, and the crowd reacted as if it knew this might be the only time it would ever get to cheer the running back from Syracuse.

"I get goose bumps thinking about it even now," Morton said.

After the last game played in the old stadium, a 26–10 victory over the Cincinnati Bengals on December 17, 1995, Morton remembers watching fans with tears streaming down their faces pull out chain saws to cut out seats.

Morton didn't saw away any seats. But his wife, Emily, bought him two commemorative bricks that are on display in the plaza outside the new stadium. One reads, "Thanks Paul Brown." The other reads, "Geoff Morton, 50+ years in the bleachers."

The Drive

Technically speaking, of course, The Drive didn't beat the Cleveland Browns in the 1986 American Football Conference Championship game. It only felt that way.

Although Denver quarterback John Elway moved his team 98 yards in less than five minutes, his five-yard touchdown pass to rookie Mark Jackson and the subsequent kick by Rich Karlis only tied the score at 20–20 with 37 seconds left in regulation.

After the Browns offense actually lost yardage on its final possession in regulation, the Browns won the coin toss at the start of overtime. But, once again, the offense went nowhere, and after a 41-yard punt by Jeff Gossett, Elway and the Broncos started on their own 25-yard line. This time Elway, playing on a bad left ankle, moved his team 60 yards in just under five minutes, setting up an AFC-title-winning 33-yard field goal by Karlis at the 5:48 mark of overtime on January 11, 1987.

That's what beat the Browns. That's what started Elway on his path toward immortality and the Hall of Fame. A fourth-year pro at the time who had been the number one pick in the 1983 NFL draft (taken by the Baltimore Colts, who immediately traded him to Denver), Elway had his share of critics. The Drive silenced them all.

"Whenever you have John Elway as your quarterback, you've got a chance," Denver coach Dan Reeves told reporters after the game.

Browns fans were devastated. They'd barely recovered from the Browns' 23–20 double overtime victory over the New York Jets in the AFC playoffs a week earlier—their first playoff victory in 17 years. They'd watched as the defense contained Elway for the better part of the game. Stung so often—remember Red Right 88, the interception thrown by

DID YOU KNOW . . . That John Elway led the Broncos on a record 47 game-tying or game-winning fourth-quarter drives?

Brian Sipe with 41 seconds left in what became a 14–12 loss to the Oakland Raiders after the 1980 season?—they'd dared to dream of the Super Bowl. Now their dreams were dashed. Again. Instead it was the Broncos who advanced to Super Bowl XXI in the Rose Bowl in Pasadena, California, where they would face the New York Giants.

"I tried to get to Pasadena during my whole college career," Elway, a Pac-10 star at Stanford, told reporters after the game. "Now I'm finally going." Just as in Cleveland on that cold January afternoon, he led the way.

Elway's heroics started after the Browns had taken a 20–13 lead on a 48-yard touchdown pass from Bernie Kosar to Brian Brennan. The Broncos muffed the kickoff and started The Drive on their own 2-yard line with 5:32 left in regulation. "I told them we had plenty of time," Reeves told reporters after the game. "I told them to go out and execute and not worry about the situation."

Elway told reporters, "We play best when our backs are to the wall. Our backs couldn't get closer to the wall than the 2-yard line."

Denver wide receiver Steve Watson told reporters that Elway came to the huddle wearing a cocky smile and said, "If you work hard, good things are going to happen."

The Drive started slowly. First Elway passed for five yards to Sammy Winder.

"That gave us some breathing room," Reeves said later.

Then Winder took a pitchout and ran three yards. After a Denver timeout, Winder ran two yards over left guard and then three yards over left tackle. On second-and-seven, Elway was flushed out of the pocket and scrambled for 11 yards. On first-and-10 at the Denver 26, Elway threw a 22-yard pass to Steve Sewell and then a 12-yard pass to Watson to move into Cleveland territory at the 40.

Elway's next pass fell incomplete; then Dave Puzzuoli sacked Elway for an eight-yard loss. That took the game to third-and-18 at the Cleveland 48. After a timeout, the unflappable Elway hit Jackson for a 20-yard gain.

"There were two options on the play," Reeves told reporters after the game. "John had one receiver out seven or eight yards and another about 20. I told him if the short man was open, don't pass him up because we still have fourth down, but [Clay] Matthews had him pretty well tied up. I don't know who was on Mark. They rolled over in a zone and he was open."

For Browns coach Marty Schottenheimer, that was the biggest of the Broncos' big plays. "There were others, but that may have been the most important," the coach said after the game.

After another incomplete pass, Elway hit Sewell for 14 yards to move to the Cleveland 14. After another completion, Elway ran for nine yards. On third-and-one from the Cleveland 5, Elway found Jackson in the end zone and Karlis's kick tied the game with 37 seconds left in regulation. Of his touchdown, Jackson said, "I saw no pressure on John at all. I thought, 'This is six for sure.'"

The stunned Browns won the coin toss in overtime. Bernie Kosar ran for two yards and passed to Brennan for six more, but on third-and-two at the Cleveland 38 Herman Fontenot was stopped by Karl Mecklenberg for no gain. "I was trying to get outside, to turn it up," Fontenot told reporters after the game.

After Gossett's punt, Denver started on its own 25. Winder ran for three yards, and Elway passed to Orson Mobley for 22 yards. Winder lost two yards, and then Sam Clancy got his hand on Elway's next lob pass. "If I had taken another step backward, I think I would have had it," Clancy told reporters after the game. Instead, on third-and-12 from the 50, Elway scrambled left and passed 28 yards to Watson. "I got around Hanford [Dixon] with a pretty clean release," Watson told reporters after the game. "The mistake he made was he released me after he saw John move out of the pocket. When John rolled toward us, Dixon came up and the safety [Felix Wright] didn't get over quick enough. So I split the difference between the two of them and John laid it up.

"I'm the third receiver in the pattern. Dixon had me man-to-man. He was with me for a while, but he released

TRIVIA

How many penalties were committed during the 1986 AFC Championship game?

Answers to the trivia questions are on pages 159–160.

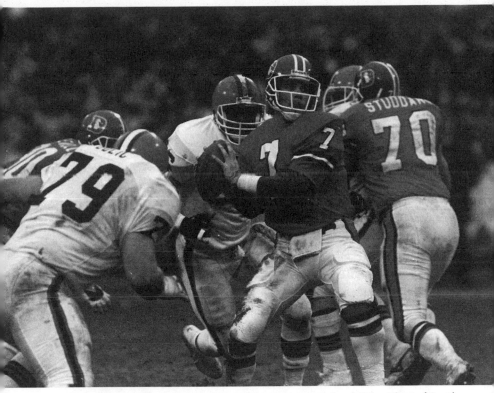

Browns fans still shudder at the thought of Denver quarterback John Elway (No. 7) and his dominance in the 1986 AFC Championship game.

me. He's one of the best defensive backs I've played against. He definitely deserves to go to the Pro Bowl, but every once in a while you get the little break you need, and that's my game."

Said Wright after the game, "We were in zone coverage. If I hadn't slipped on the play, I would have got to the ball. We have no excuses. We weren't tired. We were excited. We never thought they'd go 98 yards to tie it."

On first-and-10 at the Cleveland 22, three runs by Winder moved the ball to the Cleveland 15, setting the stage for Karlis's 33-yard field goal. "I made it by about a foot inside that left post," Karlis, a University of Cincinnati alumnus who grew up in Salem, Ohio, near Youngstown, told reporters after the game. "I was so worried. The dirt was so sandy. All

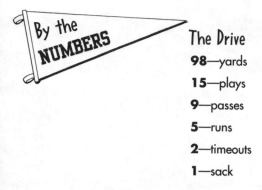

The Drive

98—yards

15—plays

9—passes

5—runs

2—timeouts

1—sack

they had done was scrape grass clippings over it. I was looking for a good place to kick it from. Finally, I just said, 'The heck with it.'"

Said Reeves after the game, "The way we did it, it was so awesome. It's my biggest thrill as a coach. It's almost like a Hollywood script."

On those last two drives Elway threw for 128 yards and ran for 20. "They were the greatest drives I've ever been involved with," he told reporters.

"That's the great thing about John," Watson told reporters after the game. "The ball gets there before anybody has a chance to react. ... He can do anything. He can throw off his back foot, the front foot, running backwards, running sideways. We've seen him do things this year and then you go back and look at them on film and you can't believe he did them."

The Browns, of course, could not believe it either. Some questioned the game plan.

Said safety Chris Rockins to reporters, "When you get a quarterback like Elway who can scramble, three guys are not going to be able to rush him. It hurt us. Every time I looked back, he was running somewhere. I'm pretty sure we would have stopped them if we had rushed four men. We rushed four men most of the game. That's what happens when you go away from your game plan. When they're 98 yards away, you should stop them."

Said Schottenheimer in reply, "We definitely did not change our defense. We were mixing our coverages just as we had through the entire game. There was man-to-man, some zone, and a four-man line part of the time. Give them credit. My hat is off to them. They made the plays when they had to."

Dixon was writing a column titled Dawg Diary for *The Plain Dealer* at the time. He spoke for the 79,915 fans who saw what they still wish they hadn't when he wrote, "When Rich Karlis got ready to kick the field goal, I didn't look. I closed my eyes. I crossed my fingers and started praying.

"When I looked up and saw the officials rule it good, I can't explain the feeling. It was almost like I didn't want to play football anymore. I don't ever want that feeling again."

The Fumble

After Denver quarterback John Elway engineered The Drive en route to leading the Broncos to a 23–20 overtime victory over the Browns in the 1986 AFC Championship game, Cleveland coach Marty Schottenheimer tried to console his team and his fans.

"There's a tremendous disappointment you are faced with, but our football team has shown great character and will be back," Schottenheimer told reporters after the game. "I told them I knew how disappointed they were in that first flush of defeat. I believed we would win and am just as disappointed as anyone. I particularly feel bad because of the great fan support we've had. I also told the squad to remember that we would be back."

Schottenheimer had said the same thing after the Browns lost 24–21 to the Miami Dolphins in an AFC divisional playoff game after the 1985 season.

"I told them then that we would be back, and we were," Schottenheimer said. "I'll say it again that this football team is not finished. We will be back."

Unfortunately for the Browns, Elway and the Broncos were back, too. They had failed in their bid to win the Super Bowl against the New York Giants, losing 39–20, so they were just as hungry as the Browns were to correct what went wrong at the end of their previous season.

This time the Broncos didn't need an awe-inspiring effort by Elway or an overtime period. On January 17, 1988, in the 1987 AFC Championship game, they beat the visiting Browns 38–33 when Earnest Byner fumbled just short of the goal line while trying to score a game-tying touchdown with 1:05 left. On second-and-five at the Broncos' 8, Byner picked up seven yards before Denver backup cornerback Jeremiah

Brian Brennan (No. 86) consoles Earnest Byner after The Fumble.

DID YOU KNOW . . .

That after yet another heart-wrenching playoff loss to the Broncos, things went from bad to worse for the Browns? Their charter plane was scheduled to leave Denver at about 8:30 PM, but mechanical difficulties prevented it from becoming airborne. While preparing to take off, the crew noticed a problem in the number two engine of the three-engine aircraft. Crash and fire equipment were called out, but the plane taxied back to the gate without incident. Five hours later it took off for the three-hour flight home. About 1,000 fans were waiting for the players upon their return.

Castille stripped the ball from Byner at the 1-yard line and recovered it at the 3-yard line. Four plays later Denver punter Mike Horan ran out of the end zone for a meaningless safety with eight seconds left.

"I broke to the outside and cut between two guys and the ball came out," Byner told reporters after the game. "I should have tucked it in more."

Thus ended a drive that might have rivaled that of Elway's a year earlier and would have capped an unbelievable comeback for the Browns.

Denver had jumped out to a 21–3 lead in the first half, turning three turnovers into three touchdowns. Safety Felix Wright picked off an interception on the first series of the second half, and three plays later Bernie Kosar called an audible and threw an 18-yard touchdown pass to Reggie Langhorne. After an 80-yard touchdown by Mark Jackson restored the Broncos' lead to 28–10 with 3:57 left in the third quarter, Byner scored on a 32-yard pass play and a four-yard run as the Browns closed the score to 28–24. The Browns had scored 21 points in six minutes and 38 seconds.

Rich Karlis, whose 33-yard field goal in overtime had beaten the Browns a year earlier, hit a 38-yarder as Denver's lead increased to 31–24. Byner's 53-yard run set up a four-yard touchdown pass from Kosar to Webster Slaughter that tied the score at 31–31.

Of course, Elway was not done. His screen pass to Sammy Winder went for 20 yards and a touchdown to give Denver a 38–31 lead with 4:01 left.

The Browns started their final push on their own 25 with 3:53 left. Having watched Kosar lead the Browns to four touchdowns in the second half, the Broncos were worried they might end up on the wrong end of The Drive this time. "I thought I'd be looking at another 90-yard drive," Elway admitted to reporters after the game.

Kosar needed 75 yards, and he got about 74 before the bottom once again fell out for the Browns. As a triumphant Castille jogged off the field and he and his teammates prepared to face the Washington Redskins in the Super Bowl, a stunned Byner stood in the end zone while teammates tried to console him. They would defend him when talking to reporters later.

"Earnest is, without a doubt, one of the classiest and best all-around players in the NFL," Kosar said. "Without a doubt, he was one of the main reasons that we were here today. It's just unfortunate that something like this happened, but there isn't any one play that wins or loses a football game."

Schottenheimer was near tears when he said, "I told Earnest that this football team would not be in the position it was today without him. His heroics, the kind of game he had, was what put us in the position to win."

Kosar put his arm around Byner on the sideline. "I said I felt bad for him and that I knew that play did not lose this game for us," said Kosar, who completed 26 of 41 passes for 356 yards and three touchdowns.

That said, the loss still hurt. "Words can't really describe the feelings, as bad as our team feels right now," Kosar said. "It's tough to come back and tie the game and then lose. It's not fun losing this game, much less two years in a row."

Added tight end Ozzie Newsome, "You don't get too many opportunities in life to get a second chance. For us to get into the championship game a second time, for us to fall behind and fight back and then lose it—well, it hurts twice as much.

"All week long the one thing we stressed was that we couldn't turn the ball over to them. We knew their defense practiced 10, 15 minutes every day stripping the ball from the runners and receivers. So what do we do? We turn the ball over twice early and they score."

By the NUMBERS

$18,000—Playoff share for Browns and Broncos players

$9,000—Playoff share for the replacement players who participated in three games while the NFL players were on strike at the start of the season

The most unusual responses on the fumble that day came from the player who fumbled and the player who forced the fumble. Perhaps both were in shock.

Byner told reporters, "It didn't hurt me as much as the Indianapolis game because I know I gave it everything I had today," he said, referring to a goal-line fumble in a 9–7 loss to the Colts on December 6. "I left everything on the field."

Indeed, he finished with 67 yards rushing, 120 yards receiving, and two touchdowns. But when pressed about his first comment, Byner seemed upset.

"I'm not in great spirits," he said. "What am I supposed to do? I'm being a man about it. I left everything I had on that field today. I won't be a baby about it. I'm not going to stand up here and cry and feel sorry for myself and my teammates. All I can do is work harder and try to get here again. The guys on this team are great people and we're going to work harder and harder. It was a tough loss. We overcame a lot of adversity to get where we got."

Castille declined to comment to reporters and said he wasn't talking until the Super Bowl.

A Punishing Runner and a Brown at Heart: Kevin Mack

The heavy gray clouds hung low over Cleveland Browns Stadium. The wind howled off the lake, and the snowflakes felt like little needles when they hit exposed flesh. It was exactly the kind of day opponents expect in Cleveland in December.

Kevin Mack stood on the sideline, beaming. He wore a long wool coat but no hat, and the snowflakes formed little droplets on his glasses. He looked like a happy man.

It had been 20 years since he rushed for 1,104 yards as a rookie in 1985 and a dozen years since he retired in 1993. As a rookie he had to be convinced he was good enough to play in the National Football League, and his ending with the Browns was not a good one. He had survived The Drive and The Fumble and an embarrassing arrest for drugs. But on this December afternoon none of that mattered. For the first time, Mack was going to meet the great Jim Brown.

"When I first got here in 1985, I learned a lot about the tradition of the team and the players they had," Mack recalled. "It was a big thing. The biggest name I heard when I got here was Jim Brown. Everybody knew who he was. So it was like following in footsteps. They were big footsteps to fill, but I just wanted to go out and do the best I could to keep the tradition alive."

In his nine years with the Browns, Mack never had a chance to meet the man whose record—for rushing yards by a rookie—he'd broken. It hadn't happened in the intervening 12 years either.

But with Browns running back Reuben Droughns poised to reach the 1,000-yard mark and become the first Brown to rush for 1,000 yards in a season since Mack and Earnest Byner became the third pair of NFL

Kevin Mack (No. 34) was a powerful back who ran into trouble but recovered nicely. Photo courtesy of Getty Images.

teammates to do so in 1985, Mack and Brown were among those invited back to celebrate the feat. (Byner, now a coach with the Washington Redskins, was also invited, but he had a game to attend.)

Before the game, Mack met The Man.

"I was trying to be cool and keep my emotions under wraps," Mack said, laughing. "But it was good. I was like a kid in a candy store. He and I walked down along the sidelines. We met the owner, Randy Lerner. The whole time we were walking down, I stayed one step behind him. It was like, 'I'm with Jim.'"

The visit brought back some warm memories for Mack, and he figured it was the perfect day for a Browns rusher to reach a milestone. "With the tradition of the Browns and the time of year it is—it's going to be cold and a little wet from the snow—it's living up to the hard-nosed mystique of being a Browns running back," Mack said.

Mack did just that in his nine seasons with the team. Although he never again reached the 1,000-yard mark after his rookie season, he was a punishing runner for the Browns, just as he had been at Kings Mountain High School in North Carolina, where he gained 1,585 yards as a senior, and Clemson, where his 862 yards as a senior in 1983 ranked fourth among NCAA fullbacks. He also played on Clemson's 1981 national championship team, which went 12–0 and beat Nebraska 22–15 in the Orange Bowl.

Feeling unready for the NFL, Mack played for Los Angeles in the USFL in 1984 before joining the Browns in 1985. If he was surprised by his success running the football that season, he was stunned when no other Brown managed to run for 1,000 yards until Droughns did it in 2005.

"It's hard to believe," Mack said. "Twenty years? You never think as a player it's going to take 20 years for somebody to do something, especially with the tradition of the team having great running backs. Not to have a 1,000-yard rusher is a sin."

Even though he lives in Houston, where he runs a moving company, Cleveland is never far from Mack's

TRIVIA

Who were the first two pairs of running backs to rush for 1,000 yards in one season?

Answers to the trivia questions are on pages 159–160.

TOP FIVE

Most Rushing Touchdowns in Browns Career (NFL games)

1.	106	Jim Brown	1957–65
2.	74	Leroy Kelly	1964–73
3.	47	Mike Pruitt	1976–84
4.	46	Kevin Mack	1985–93
5.	33	Otto Graham	1950–55

mind during the football season. That's partly because inevitably someone will call him after seeing a replay of The Drive or The Fumble on television. He explained:

It's amazing. Every time those games come on, somebody calls my house and says, "Hey, you're on TV." They're showing The Drive or The Fumble. It's gotten to the point now where it's just kind of numbing to hear about it. I tell folks, "I don't want to hear about it. I don't want to see it. I was there."

It was a hard time. The three AFC Championship games were hard. It was bitter. They all went right down to the end. I was glad I was there. I'm glad our team was there. We played great in all three of those seasons, and I think the fans enjoyed our play in those years, even though we didn't make it to our ultimate goal of being in the Super Bowl.

There were other hard times for Mack in Cleveland. He spent 30 days in prison in 1989 after pleading guilty to cocaine abuse. By the time he returned to the team, the Browns were fighting to make the playoffs. On one memorable play against Houston in the last regular-season game on December 23, 1989, Mack dragged three defenders four yards into the end zone, scoring the touchdown that gave the Browns a 24–20 victory. After the game he sobbed in the arms of owner Art Modell.

Mack was set to retire in 1993, but he changed his mind. Unfortunately, Coach Bill Belichick chose not to use him much, and he didn't get even one carry in Cleveland's Municipal Stadium in his last game.

But Mack holds no grudges.

"I had a great time here," he said. "Unfortunately, when I left, the team was in transition. We had a new coach, and he was trying to bring in his own people and personnel, which is understandable. That's just the nature of the beast. It's the way the game goes. I was caught on the bad side of that. It was his first head coaching job, so he was really just learning how to be a head coach."

If his career didn't end quite the way he had hoped, Mack remained a Brown in his heart.

"Cleveland is the only team I ever really played for," he said. "I never considered myself not a Brown."

The King of Cleveland— Bernie Kosar

Bernie Kosar and the Cleveland Browns have come full circle.

After a painful parting and a number of difficult years, the Ohio native who grew up as a Browns fan is once again back in the fold. During the 2005 season Kosar served as a mentor for rookie quarterback Charlie Frye, much as quarterback Gary Danielson served as a mentor for Kosar in his rookie season with the Browns in 1985.

Kosar and Frye had much in common. Kosar grew up as a Browns fan in Boardman, Ohio, outside Youngstown. He had Browns posters on the wall in his room, and he wore Brian Sipe's No. 17 jersey. Frye grew up in Willard, Ohio, south of Sandusky, and he had posters of Kosar in his room at home. Still does, in fact.

That was the norm for kids (and adults) growing up in Ohio in the 1980s, when Kosar was king. He'd been the Associated Press Player of the Year as a senior at Boardman High School and wanted to attend Ohio State or Pitt, but his weird sidearm delivery scared away college coaches. He wound up at Miami and promptly led the Hurricanes to an NCAA title with an upset of Nebraska in the Orange Bowl after the 1983 season.

At 6'5" and 210 pounds, he was slow, but he was smart and had great vision, which made him the darling of pro football scouts. In fact when Kosar left Miami with two years of eligibility remaining, there was so much jostling for draft position that the NFL actually had to rule on which team owned his rights. Houston and Minnesota had worked out a deal that would have given Minnesota the number one pick in the regular draft, but Cleveland and Buffalo had worked out a deal that gave Cleveland the number one pick in the supplemental draft. Cleveland traded first and third picks in the 1985 draft plus first and sixth picks in the 1986 draft to Buffalo for the number one pick in the supplemental draft. When word got out that the NFL was about to rule in favor of the Browns, there were so many calls to *The Plain Dealer* switchboard that the whole phone system shut down for a time.

Kosar reported to Coach Marty Schottenheimer's training camp eager to learn from Danielson, and the two formed a strong bond, much like the one that would someday form between Kosar and Frye. But when Danielson was injured, Kosar was forced into the lineup against the New England Patriots during the fifth week of the season.

Beloved quarterback Bernie Kosar throws against the Denver Broncos in 1993.

He got off to an inauspicious start, fumbling his first snap. But he quickly made good, completing seven straight passes to lead the Browns to a 24–20 victory. With Kosar behind center the Browns went 8–8 that season and made their first of five straight playoff appearances, falling 24–21 to the Miami Dolphins. The Browns vaulted to a 12–4 record the next season, when Kosar threw for 3,854 yards and 17 touchdowns. In 1987 Kosar had 22 touchdowns and only nine interceptions, completing an NFL-best 62 percent of his passes for an AFC-best 95.4 quarterback rating.

Of course, both of those seasons ended with excruciating losses to John Elway and the Denver Broncos in the AFC Championship game, as did the 1989 season, when Kosar threw for 3,533 yards and 18 touchdowns. Elway and the Broncos blocked Kosar and the Browns from reaching the Super Bowl three times.

Kosar injured his elbow in the 1988 season opener at Kansas City, and some observers think he was never the same after that injury. He missed seven games in 1988, Schottenheimer's last year as the Browns coach, but came back strong for Coach Bud Carson in 1989. Then came the disastrous 1990 season. Kosar threw 15 interceptions and 10 touchdowns as the Browns finished 3–13. His numbers were better in 1991, when Bill Belichick replaced Carson. Kosar threw for 3,487 yards and 18 touchdowns with nine interceptions, but the Browns were just 6–10 in 1991 and 7–9 in 1992.

By 1993 things were beginning to unravel on a number of fronts. In his book on Belichick, *The Education of a Coach*, author David Halberstam wrote of Belichick's time in Cleveland, "Everything that could go wrong did go wrong."

The team was struggling and had not made the playoffs since 1989, which didn't sit well with fans. Reporters were growing increasingly tired of dealing with Belichick, a disciple of the controlling Bill Parcells. Not only did Belichick come across as colorless at best and belligerent at worst, but assistant coaches were off-limits for interviews and players were available only at certain times, quite a shock for a press corps that had enjoyed fairly open access.

All that was bad enough, but then Belichick committed a cardinal sin in the minds of loyal Cleveland fans: he messed with Kosar. Fans still saw the quarterback as one of their own. They identified with Kosar more than they ever had with the coach.

Bill Livingston has been a sports columnist at *The Plain Dealer* for 21 years, and he thinks Kosar is the most popular player he has covered during his time in Cleveland.

"First of all, Bernie wanted this inferiority complex ridden city," Livingston said. "He manipulated the draft to come here. He was also the epitome of the ugly duckling overachiever vs. the golden boy—John Elway—who didn't want to play for a bad team [Baltimore at the time] and forced a trade."

The Browns started 5–2 in 1993. After throwing a touchdown pass to Michael Jackson in a 23–13 victory over visiting San Francisco in a *Monday Night Football* game on September 13, Kosar came off the field and immediately got into it with Belichick on the sideline. The coach was upset that Kosar had changed the play Belichick had sent in.

Kosar lost his starting job to Vinny Testaverde, but an injury put him back at the helm against visiting Denver on November 7. The final straw for Belichick apparently came after Kosar drew up a play in the dirt that resulted in a 33-yard touchdown for Jackson. Once again Belichick was irate, and it was more than the 29–14 loss to the Broncos that upset him. It was a question of who was in charge of the team.

Many players were loyal to Kosar, and there was a sense that the two could not coexist. Owner Art Modell had vowed that Belichick was the last coach he'd ever hire and that if it didn't work, he'd get out of football. That left him little wiggle room. Modell also brought in former Browns star running back Jim Brown to help Belichick in the locker room, and Brown was also of the opinion that Kosar's skills were diminishing and that having him on the team could only lead to a split locker room.

TRIVIA

In what subject did
Bernie Kosar earn his
degrees from the
University of Miami?

Answers to the trivia questions are on pages 159–160.

 **Browns Records Still Held by Bernie Kosar**

308—Consecutive passes without an interception (NFL record)

2.57—Lowest career interception percentage (minimum 750 attempts)

1.82—Lowest season interception percentage (minimum 200 attempts)

So after meeting long into the night after that loss to Denver, the Browns announced on Monday, November 8, 1993, that they were releasing Kosar because of his diminishing skills. The city of Cleveland was outraged. The Dawgs howled long and loud, and their loyalties were tested when Kosar signed with the Dallas Cowboys later that week. In fact, for a time Kosar's new Dallas jersey outsold those of longtime Dallas stars Troy Aikman, Emmitt Smith, and Michael Irvin, and by the end of the next Browns game, a 22–5 loss at Seattle with Todd Philcox at quarterback, twice as many Cleveland televisions were tuned to the Dallas game.

Kosar won a Super Bowl ring as a backup for the Cowboys that season, and he played behind Dan Marino for three seasons in Miami before retiring in 1996. He tried to remain involved with the Browns in various ways during their hiatus and return, even attempting to become part of one of the ownership groups whose bid was ultimately rejected in favor of the late Al Lerner's. But the Carmen Policy regime never seemed to embrace him the way the fans and the media hoped it would.

In some ways, Browns fans never really got over Kosar's departure. And then, two years later, Modell moved the team to Baltimore—without Belichick. Belichick was hired as head coach of New England on January 27, 2000, and led the Patriots to three Super Bowl victories in four years by 2004.

After one of the New England Patriots' Super Bowl championships, Belichick was asked what he'd learned in Cleveland. "Not to move your team to another city in the middle of the season," he said.

If only he'd shown the same sense of timing and good humor with the Browns, things might have ended differently in Cleveland for him, for Kosar, and for the whole team.

A City Abandoned

The official end came on November 6, 1995, when Cleveland Browns owner Art Modell announced he was accepting a sweetheart deal from Maryland and moving his team to Baltimore. "I had no choice," said Modell.

Those four words broke millions of hearts. Instead of celebrating the golden anniversary of a legendary franchise in 1996, Browns fans were left out in the cold. A cartoon caricature of Modell was pictured on the cover of *Sports Illustrated* sucker punching a hound dog wearing a Browns jersey and helmet, no doubt an accurate representation of how the fans felt.

Outraged voices rose from all corners—not just in Cleveland but around the country. From crying fans on the street in front of the old Municipal Stadium to newspaper editorial writers to national television commentators like Bob Costas, everybody portrayed Modell as a villain.

Although he had been quoted in 1994 saying that he would not move the team even if he did not get a new or remodeled stadium, Modell started meeting with Maryland officials in the summer of 1995. With mounting debts, how could he pass up a rent-free, $200-million new stadium and the rights to sell $80-million worth of personal seat licenses?

Rumors of the move first appeared in newspapers a few days before the official announcement, but there had been signs of trouble long before that—more than a dozen years earlier, in fact. In the early 1980s, after the Browns took over the operation of the stadium, Modell was involved in costly lawsuits with the Indians and Browns' minority owner Bob Gries. In addition, the National Football League players went on strike in 1982 and 1987. So stressful were things in the 1980s that Modell, previously diagnosed with a bleeding ulcer, suffered a heart attack and needed quadruple bypass surgery. Complications arose, and it took him most of the summer of 1983 to recover.

After the second players strike in 1987 things got worse on and off the field. Despite the fact that Modell pledged $10 million in capital improvements to the stadium, the city council refused to grant the stadium corporation a 10-year lease extension. Meanwhile, the Gateway Corporation was formed, which would lead to the Indians leaving Municipal Stadium and moving into their own brand-new digs—right across the street from the Cavaliers, who were leaving the Richfield Coliseum for the brand-new Gund Arena. Those teams were getting a great deal. They retained the rights to revenues, while the Gateway

Browns fans took their seats home after the last game at Cleveland Municipal Stadium in 1995. Photo courtesy of Diamond Images.

DID YOU KNOW . . . That Art Modell finalized his deal with the Maryland Stadium Authority aboard the private jet of Al Lerner? Lerner, a minority owner of the Browns at the time, eventually bought the new Browns team for a record $530 million, succeeding Modell as owner.

Corporation agreed to fund all capital improvements. The project was funded by a sin tax on cigarettes and alcohol. At one point Modell was quoted as saying, "Give me the same deal the city gave [Indians owner] Dick Jacobs and I'll be a happy camper."

Modell suffered additional health problems and eventually had a second open-heart surgery, followed three years later by hip surgery. It did not make him feel any better when the Browns finished with an all-time worst record of 3–13 in 1990. With the lawsuits, the strikes, the payments to coaches who had been fired in addition to those actually coaching, the failure of players to perform up to their potential, and the constant upkeep of a field damaged by concerts and other events held there, Modell was hemorrhaging money. In 1992 a story in *The Plain Dealer* revealed that the Browns had suffered $12 million in losses over a 10-year period.

Still, Modell said he wanted to work things out and stay in Cleveland, although relations with the media and elected officials were increasingly hostile. In late 1994, then Cleveland mayor Michael White said the stadium was a top priority, and he warned that if the city did not come through with an estimated $130 million needed for renovations, he feared Modell would sell or move the team. For taxpayers still trying to swallow the Gateway deal, it was a tough sell.

Looking back, it should have been no surprise that the team raised prices for the 1995 season. But Modell expected great things from his team that year. That, he said, was part of the reason he decided to place a moratorium on discussions of the stadium renovation, now projected to run $175 million. He wanted the focus on his team and the game. He didn't break the moratorium even when Cuyahoga County commissioners put the sin tax extension on the November ballot.

With frequent delays and no actual plan forthcoming from the mayor, Modell began discussions with Baltimore, which eventually led to that painful announcement on November 6. Ironically, the extension

Scoring in the Final Season in Municipal Stadium

113 points—Matt Stover

54 points—Michael Jackson

24 points—Keenan McCardell and Earnest Byner

18 points—Andre Rison

12 points—Vinny Testeverde

6 points—Walter Reeves, Derrick Alexander, Rico Smith, Mike Caldwell, Gerald Dixon, Frank Hartley, and Lorenzo White

2 points—Eric Zeier

of the sin tax passed on November 7. That kick-started the "Save Our Browns" campaign as the city and Browns fans vowed they were not giving up their team without a fight. They obtained a restraining order blocking the move. NFL owners, scheduled to meet in Atlanta in January, were besieged with phone calls and faxes from Browns fans, who staged rallies whenever and wherever they thought they could attract attention.

The unprecedented campaign succeeded. On December 10, 1995, National Football League Commissioner Paul Tagliabue said, "I think our challenge is to keep a team in Cleveland and get a team to Baltimore. We're going to respect the fans. We'll stick with those fans and we'll find a way to get that done. The specifics are what we're working on now."

The question was whether Cleveland would get a relocated team or an expansion team. Eventually the league decided on an expansion team, pleasing those who wanted to prevent another city from going through the heartbreak Browns fans had experienced. Tagliabue allowed Modell to move his team, but the Browns' name and history were to remain in Cleveland. (Those close to Modell, a man who'd been stung by the relocation of the Brooklyn Dodgers to Los Angeles as a youth, say he intended to leave behind the team's name, colors, and history all along.)

In the middle of all this the 1995 Browns team suffered through an incredibly difficult season. They were 4–4 when the rumors started. They lost a home game to the Houston Oilers the day before Modell's announcement. That was the start of a six-game losing streak during which the fans booed the players (and the absent owner) unmercifully.

In their last game at Cleveland's Municipal Stadium, on December 17, the Browns beat the Cincinnati Bengals 26–10. During the game many fans displayed signs critical of Modell, and some started to destroy parts of the stadium, ripping out benches just as their own hearts had been ripped out.

TRIVIA

Which other National Football League team had the city of Baltimore approached before reaching a deal with Cleveland owner Art Modell?

Answers to the trivia questions are on pages 159–160.

But then a wonderful thing happened. At the end of the game many of the players headed for the Dawg Pound to say good-bye and thank you to the fans who had supported them so loyally for so long. There were not many dry eyes in the stadium by the end of the afternoon.

Modell's move did pay dividends for him. His Baltimore Ravens won the Super Bowl after the 2000 season. He sold the team in 2003 for $600 million.

The Browns Are Back

It has been 10 years since Art Modell moved his team to Baltimore, and seven years since the expansion Browns returned to Cleveland. But somehow things haven't quite worked out exactly the way Browns fans had hoped they would.

True, they have their own team to cheer for again and a gleaming new stadium. Unfortunately, there hasn't been a whole heck of a lot to cheer for since the team returned. In fact, the 2005 season marked the third phase in the team's rebuilding mode.

When fans bombarded the offices of NFL Commissioner Paul Tagliabue and NFL owners in the wake of Modell's announcement, the league responded to their anguish. It allowed Modell to move his team. But the Browns' name, colors, and history remained in Cleveland. True to their word, NFL executives arranged for an expansion team to begin play in Cleveland in 1999.

The decrepit Cleveland Municipal Stadium was torn down in 1996—after more than 65,000 fans took advantage of a final viewing promotion entitled "The Final Play." Ground was broken for the 73,200-seat open-air Cleveland Browns Stadium on May 15, 1997, on the site of the old stadium on Cleveland's lakefront, next to the Rock and Roll Hall of Fame and the Great Lakes Science Center. Five months later 52,000 season tickets had been sold for a stadium that would eventually cost $290 million.

In the meantime a very public courtship took place as six opportunistic groups bid to become the owners of the new team. Multimillionaires joined forces with retired athletes and wealthy celebrities in an effort to persuade the NFL of their worthiness. Real estate developer Bart Wolstein teamed with former Browns players Jim Brown, Dick Schafrath, and Mike McCormack, while Cablevision founder Charles Dolan and his brother, attorney Lawrence Dolan, paired with comedian Bill Cosby and former Miami head coach Don Shula, an Ohio native.

In the end the NFL chose Alfred Lerner—whose MBNA Corporation, a credit card giant, had made him one of the wealthiest men in the country—and Carmen Policy, a Youngstown, Ohio, native who had helped the San Francisco 49ers build a dynasty that won five NFL championships. The selling price was an astounding $530 million, a record at the time.

The new owners' first move was to hire another former San Francisco star and executive, Dwight Clark, as vice president, director of football operations.

Next the team had to find a coach and some players. The coaching search was a public one, played out in the media. It actually started with a misstep when Policy mentioned at a luncheon that Mike Holmgren

Fireworks in Cleveland Browns Stadium signal the team's return in 1999.

would make a fine coach for the Browns. Unfortunately for Policy, Holmgren was still coach of the Green Bay Packers at the time, although he reportedly had been thinking about leaving. That slip of the lip led to a charge of "tampering" and a $10,000 fine from the NFL.

But there were plenty of coaches who were actually available after the season. There was Brian Billick, offensive coordinator of the Minnesota Vikings, a team coming off a 15–1 season. Another option was Gary Kubiak, offensive coordinator for the Denver Broncos during their two Super Bowls. Also on the table was Art Shell, former head coach of the Los Angeles Raiders who had become offensive line coach for the NFC champion Atlanta Falcons. There was Willie Shaw, the Raiders' defensive coordinator who had worked under Tony Dungy in Minnesota. Last but not least was Jacksonville offensive coordinator Chris Palmer, who had a great reputation for working with young quarterbacks.

The rumor mill first seemed to favor Kubiak, who eventually elected to stay in Denver. Then Billick, who rubbed some people the wrong way with what they perceived as arrogance, withdrew from consideration. Adding insult to injury, he was then named coach of Modell's team, now the Baltimore Ravens. So the Browns turned to Palmer, who became the first coach of the new Browns on January 21, 1999.

With six months until the start of training camp and a clock on Cleveland's downtown Tower City landmark ticking down the days until the start of the season, the Browns started acquiring players and coaches. The big day was February 9, 1999, when the team picked 37 players in the expansion draft, including 28-year-old guard Jim Pyne, who had started every game for the Detroit Lions in 1998.

Next up was the NFL draft in April. Once again the Browns conducted a very public discussion about what they planned to do with their number one pick. Sometimes they were in love with Kentucky quarterback Tim Couch. Then Oregon quarterback Akili Smith seemed to be their favorite. All the while, running back Ricky Williams of Texas remained another option.

TRIVIA

Who were the first players obtained by Carmen Policy for the new Browns?

Answers to the trivia questions are on pages 159–160.

They finally settled on Couch. In the second round they took wide receiver Kevin Johnson of Syracuse, figuring they had an explosive combination in Couch

DID YOU KNOW . . . That the only person other than kicker Phil Dawson to lead the new Browns in scoring from their return in 1999 to 2005 was running back Terry Kirby, who had 54 points to Dawson's 53 in 1999?

and Johnson that would be together for many seasons to come. Sadly, both players were gone in five years.

The season was full of firsts for the new team. The first game—and first win—came in a 20–17 victory over Dallas in the annual preseason Hall of Fame Game in Canton's Fawcett Stadium on August 9. The first game in their own new stadium was a 24–17 loss to the Minnesota Vikings in a preseason contest on August 21. The first regular-season game, which was also the first regular-season game at the new stadium, was a downer, as the Browns lost to the archrival Pittsburgh Steelers 43–0 on September 12. The first victory didn't come until Couch threw a last-second Hail Mary pass to Johnson at New Orleans on October 31. The fans would actually have to wait until the next season for the first victory in the new stadium.

After finishing 2–14 in 1999 the Browns took Penn State defensive end Courtney Brown with the first pick in the 2000 draft, hoping to start a defensive foundation to match the offensive foundation they felt they'd laid in 1999. But things did not improve significantly on either side of the ball that season, although the team did register their first win in Cleveland Browns Stadium with a satisfying 23–20 victory over those rival Steelers on September 17. Late in what would end as a 3–13 season Palmer was quoted as saying, "I feel like I'm driving a runaway train." Not long after, the Browns threw him under the bus. His two-year tenure was the shortest ever for the coach of an NFL expansion franchise.

Thus began the first rebuilding effort for the two-year-old team. Less than three weeks after firing Palmer on January 11, the Browns coronated former Dallas defensive coordinator and University of Miami coach Butch Davis as the 10th coach of the Browns franchise, the second in the new era.

The Browns' fortunes on the field improved dramatically under Davis. The team improved to 7–9 in his first season. Although they struggled to cope with the death of owner Al Lerner from brain cancer on October 23, 2002, the Browns rebounded and finished 9–7 in 2002, returning to the playoffs for the first time since the 1994 season.

By the
NUMBERS

Cleveland Browns Stadium

73,200—seats

24,703—trees, plants, and flowers

11,000—square feet of space in the Browns' locker room

10,644—Dawg Pound bleacher seats

1,436—wheelchair-accessible seats

8,754—club seats

5,600—square feet of space in each of two visiting locker rooms

640—speakers

250—media seats in main press box

147—luxury suites

83—restrooms

71—portable concession stands

41—permanent concession stands

12—ticket windows

Under backup quarterback Kelly Holcomb the Browns stormed to a 24–7 lead before Tommy Maddox led the Steelers back to a 33–28 score. On third-and-12 Dennis Northcutt dropped a pass that would have given the Browns a first down. Maddox drove the Steelers 61 yards for the game-winning touchdown and a two-point conversion in what turned out to be a 36–33 victory in the AFC wild-card game on January 5, 2003.

That would be the highlight of the Davis era. The Browns slipped back to 5–11 in 2003, and, with the team in free fall in 2004, Davis resigned after a wild 58–48 loss at Cincinnati on November 28 that left the Browns at 3–8, the fifth straight loss in what would become a nine-game losing streak. Offensive coordinator Terry Robiskie took over for the final five games of the 4–12 season.

Davis's controlling nature forced numerous changes in the Browns organization, as Clark and then Policy resigned along with a host of other staff. Couch, Johnson, and Brown were all gone, as were many of the former Miami players Davis was so fond of.

Randy Lerner replaced his father as owner of the team and hired former NFL executive John Collins as president and chief executive officer on May 1, 2004. They presided over the departure of Davis, followed by the hiring of new Senior Vice President and General Manager Phil Savage on January 7, 2005, and Coach Romeo Crennel on February 8, 2005. Thus started the second rebuilding of the new franchise.

More troubles followed. First tight end Kellen Winslow Jr., the team's first-round draft choice (number six overall) in 2004, who had missed most of his rookie season with a broken leg, suffered life-threatening injuries in an off-season motorcycle crash and missed the entire 2005 season, although he was expected back for 2006. Then rookie wide receiver Braylon Edwards, the team's first-round pick (third overall) in 2005, tore his anterior cruciate ligament and was lost for the season as the Browns stumbled to a 6–10 record, including an excruciating 41–0 loss to the visiting archrival Pittsburgh Steelers on Christmas Eve. The best news from the 2005 season seemed to be the emergence of rookie quarterback Charlie Frye from the University of Akron, the team's third-round pick in the 2005 draft. Under the tutelage of former Browns star Bernie Kosar, Frye could develop into the kind of standout quarterback Browns fans have been awaiting so patiently—although Crennel did not annoint him the starter for 2006.

At the same time a power struggle was developing that would lead to a messy ending to the 2005 campaign. Instead of celebrating a season-ending 20–16 victory over the visiting Baltimore Ravens, the Browns were scrambling to repair their fractured front office. Two days before the Baltimore game, reports surfaced that Savage—who was apparently unhappy with Collins because of changes Savage perceived as usurping his authority—was to be fired or would resign. That set up a howl of protest from fans and the media. After a shaky 72 hours, it was Collins who resigned under pressure the day after the Baltimore game. Randy Lerner said he would serve as team president until a new hire could be brought in.

Such a restructuring might not qualify as the fourth phase of the rebuilding effort that started with the team's return in 1999, but it was at the very least the second part of the third phase—with no end in sight. The patience of Browns fans was tested once again, but most remained loyal, if longing for an end to the ineptness.

Memorable Games

The Browns have been thrilling their fans since the team's inception in 1946 in the old All-America Football Conference. Trying to pick the "most" memorable games in all those years would be impossible. Each game is its own microcosm of competition and drama, memorable to participants and spectators alike. But these five regular-season games and five playoff games won't soon be forgotten by anyone who experienced them.

Regular-Season Games

At Browns 42, Chicago Bears 21 on November 25, 1951. No Browns player ever had a bigger day than wide receiver Dub Jones, who scored a team-record six touchdowns in this victory over the Bears. Jones, whose given name is William, scored on runs of two, 12, 27, and 42 yards and on receptions of 34 and 43 yards. He tied a National Football League record set by Ernie Nevers of the Chicago Cardinals in 1929 and equaled by Gale Sayers of the Chicago Bears in 1965.

 At Browns 26, Dallas 7 on September 24, 1979. The Browns were 3–0 heading into this *Monday Night Football* matchup against the defending NFC champion Cowboys. Fans started arriving downtown long before the 9:00 PM kickoff, and by the start of the game they were definitely "ready for some football," as the song goes. Longtime Browns public-address announcer Tom Glasenapp remembers struggling to be heard over the noise generated by 80,123 fans. "The crowd was crazy," Glasenapp said. "The sound guy running the system told me we were redlined and the needle was buried all night long. That meant we were as loud as we could be and still nobody could hear me." The Browns scored three touchdowns in the first seven minutes and five seconds, and the defense preserved the victory. All-Pro safety Thom Darden intercepted passes thrown by Dallas quarterback Roger Staubach twice, returning one pass 39 yards for a touchdown, and defensive tackle Jerry Sherk was credited with sacking Staubach three and one-half times. The beleaguered Dallas quarterback also fumbled twice. Browns quarterback Brian Sipe completed 15 of 28 passes for 229 yards and two touchdowns, including a 48-yard scoring pass to Ozzie Newsome.

Browns 51, at Pittsburgh 0 on September 10, 1989. Bud Carson's coaching debut was the best in the history of the NFL. Carson was 58 when he was hired by the Browns, who were determined to field a defense that could finally stop John Elway and the Denver Broncos, who'd broken the Browns' hearts in playoff games after the 1986 and 1987 seasons. Carson was the architect of the Steel Curtain defense in Pittsburgh and had also been the defensive coordinator of the Los Angeles Rams and New York Jets. The Browns were all about defense in Carson's debut against his former team and his close friend, Pittsburgh coach Chuck Noll. There was plenty of smashmouth football as the Browns forced eight turnovers and recorded seven sacks. But the defenders knew what to do with the ball when they got their hands on it, scoring three touchdowns. It was a defensive exhibition the likes of which Browns fans have not seen since.

Browns 21, at New Orleans 16 on October 31, 1999. After seven straight losses to start the new regime the Browns were in desperate need of some good news. Saints be praised, it came in the form of a Hail Mary pass from rookie quarterback Tim Couch to rookie wide receiver Kevin Johnson in the New Orleans Superdome. Trailing 16–14 with time running out, the Browns had nothing to lose on the last play of the game from their own 44-yard line. Couch, in shotgun formation, took the snap, circled right, and heaved the ball as far as he could. A Saints defender tipped it right into the hands of Johnson, who made sure he got both feet down in the right corner of the end zone. Moments later, his head, neck, shoulders, and torso followed as he and Couch were mobbed by their teammates. Meanwhile, disbelieving New Orleans coach Mike Ditka lay face down on the field. Couch called that pass a memory he'd never forget.

Jacksonville 15, at Browns 10 on December 16, 2001. This game was the Browns' lowest point since their 1999 return to Cleveland. With 48 seconds left officials used instant replay to overturn a catch by Quincy

Morgan at the Jacksonville 9-yard line. The Browns had already run another play, which usually means the preceding play cannot be reviewed, but officials said they had received an electronic signal from the replay official before the play and simply failed to stop the game in time. When the catch was overruled, giving the ball to Jacksonville, angry fans pelted the field with plastic bottles, some of which still contained beer or water. Officials, fearing for their safety and that of the players and coaches, first ruled the game over. But under orders from NFL commissioner Paul Tagliabue, the game resumed 25 minutes later. Jacksonville quarterback Mark Brunell took a knee twice against a mishmash of a defensive unit that actually included three offensive players, since most of the Browns' defense had already undressed and showered. As bad as the fans behaved, what some found most offensive was the reaction from Browns officials, who refused to criticize the unruly fans. Said Browns president Carmen Policy to reporters, "Cleveland is not going to take a black eye. Our fans had their hearts ripped out. ... I like the fact that our fans cared. ... The bottles are plastic. They don't carry much of a wallop." Owner Lerner told reporters, "Everybody controlled themselves considering they had spent 60 minutes outside in cold weather. ... It wasn't pleasant. I'm not going to suggest anything like that. But it wasn't World War III." (It must be noted that it was 44 degrees at kickoff, balmy weather in Cleveland in December.)

Playoffs

At Detroit 17, Browns 16 on December 27, 1953. In a rematch of the 1952 NFL Championship game, which halted the Browns' NFL title streak at two and their overall title streak at six, the Lions rallied to beat the Browns again. Three field goals by Lou Groza and a nine-yard run by Harry Jagade had built Cleveland a 16–10 lead with 4:10 left, despite the fact that quarterback Otto Graham had completed just two of 15 passes for 20 yards with no touchdowns and two interceptions, finishing with a quarterback rating of 0.0. Detroit quarterback Bobby Layne moved his team from its 20-yard line to the Browns' 33. Instead of running the screen play that had been called, Layne changed the play at the line of scrimmage and threw deep to Jim Doran for the winning score with 2:10 left. Doran caught three passes for 68 yards on the winning drive. The teams would meet for the championship twice

TOP FIVE

The Browns' Top Five NFL Scoring Seasons

1. 1964   415 points (22 field goals, 49 points after touchdown, 50 touchdowns)

2. 1966   403 points (nine field goals, 52 points after touchdown, 54 touchdowns)

3. 1968   394 points (18 field goals, 46 points after touchdown, 49 touchdowns)

4. 1986   391 points (26 field goals, 43 points after touchdown, 45 touchdowns)

5. 1987   390 points (21 field goals, 45 points after touchdown, 47 touchdowns)

more in the next four years, with the Browns winning in 1954 and the Lions winning again in 1957.

At Miami 20, Browns 14 on December 24, 1972. With their undefeated season on the line, the Dolphins had to rally to beat the Browns. Miami jumped off to a 10–0 lead in the first quarter on a blocked punt return and a 40-yard field goal by Garo Yepremian. The Browns got on the board in the third quarter with a five-yard run by Mike Phipps, but a 46-yard field goal by Yepremian pushed Miami's lead to 13–7 in the fourth quarter. Cleveland finally took a 14–13 lead on a 27-yard scoring pass from Phipps to Fair Hooker. But Paul Warfield caught 15- and 35-yard passes as the Dolphins drove 80 yards for the winning score, which came on an eight-yard run by Jim Kiick and a final point after touchdown by Yepremian. An interception in the closing seconds preserved the victory for Miami.

At Browns 23, New York Jets 20 in double overtime, one of five by Phipps that day, on January 3, 1987. Some consider this the greatest game the Browns have ever played. The two teams arrived at the AFC Divisional Playoff game on wildly divergent streaks. The Browns had won five straight and eight of their previous nine. The Jets had started the season 10–1 before dropping five straight. But it was the Jets who pulled out to a 13–10 lead in the fourth quarter. Bernie Kosar drove the Browns to the Jets' 2-yard line, but he forced a pass to Webster Slaughter in double coverage and was intercepted in the end zone by Russell Carter. The defense forced the Jets to punt, but Kosar threw a second interception, setting up a 25-yard scoring run by Freeman McNeil to push the Jets lead to 20–10 with 4:14 left. New York's Mark Gastineau was called for rough-ing the passer, which gave the Browns a first down on their own 33-yard line. Five passes later Kosar had moved his team to the Jets' 1-yard line at the two-minute warning. Kevin Mack rushed over the goal line to earn the Browns a 20–17 score. The defense held again, and Kosar started on the Browns' 33 with 51 seconds left. A pass interference call moved the ball to the Jets' 42. Kosar's pass glanced off the helmet of Jets cornerback Carl Howard and into the hands of Slaughter, who fell at the 5. Mark Moseley, 38 years old, who had been picked up late in the season after a knee injury to Matt Bahr, the Browns' regular kicker, hit a 22-yard field goal to send the game to overtime. Moseley missed a 23-yarder in the

Every game is a memorable one for true Browns fans, especially those in the Dawg Pound.

first overtime—his third miss of the day. But he came back with a 27-yarder just two minutes and two seconds into the second overtime to save the Browns in a four-hour game that was the third longest in NFL history. Said Coach Marty Schottenheimer to reporters after the game, "This is a victory, a game, a moment all of us will remember the rest of our lives."

TRIVIA

From the Browns' inception in the All-America Football Conference in 1946 through 2005, how many years have they missed the playoffs?

Answers to the trivia questions are on pages 159–160.

At Browns 34, Buffalo 30 on January 6, 1990. This high-scoring game was immensely entertaining. Buffalo quarterback Jim Kelly threw for 405 yards and four touchdowns, while Bernie Kosar threw for 251 yards and three scores. The Browns built a 24–14 lead in the third quarter before Kelly threw a six-yard scoring pass to Thurman Thomas to bring the score to 24–21. Rookie Eric Metcalf returned the kickoff 90 yards for a touchdown that bumped Cleveland's lead to 31–21. The teams traded field goals in the fourth quarter before Thomas scored again, this time on a three-yard pass from Kelly. But the Bills missed the extra point. Thus, on their final possession, they needed a touchdown to win instead of a field goal to tie. With the Bills driving, Clay Matthews ended the threat by picking off a Kelly pass on the 1-yard line with three seconds left. In retrospect, the Bills' loss was even more costly in that a victory might have allowed them to make five straight appearances in the Super Bowl instead of the four they made (all losses) from 1991 to 1994.

At Pittsburgh 36, Browns 33 on January 5, 2003. The AFC wild-card game was wild, all right, as the Browns returned to the postseason for the first time since their return in 1999. Kelly Holcomb started in place of the injured Tim Couch and amassed 429 yards, completing 26 of 43 passes for three touchdowns, as the Browns took a 24–7 lead with 12:11 left in the third quarter. But on this particular day, that wouldn't be enough. Tommy Maddox, the league's comeback player of the year, led the charge as the Steelers scored 29 points in the final 19 minutes of the game. The Browns still thought they were in good shape when Holcomb threw a 22-yard scoring pass to Andre Davis for a 33–21 lead with 10:17 left. But defensive penalties helped the Steelers put together a 77-yard

IF ONLY . . . The Browns had not traded Paul Warfield to the Miami Dolphins in 1970, it's possible the Dolphins would not have become the last team in professional football to have an undefeated season. It was Warfield's two clutch catches that brought the Dolphins a 20–14 victory in the AFC Divisional Playoff game on December 24, 1972.

drive that led to a five-yard touchdown pass from Maddox to Hines Ward with 3:06 left. The Browns' offense stalled, and they were facing a third-and-12 when Dennis Northcutt dropped a pass from Holcomb that would have given Cleveland a first down and a chance to pad the lead or at least run down the clock. Instead the Browns punted and the Steelers drove 61 yards, scoring on a three-yard run with 54 seconds left. After a two-point conversion Holcomb got the Browns to the Steelers' 45 with seven seconds left. But Andre King could not get out of bounds after a 16-yard reception, and time expired before the Browns could attempt a tying field goal.

Memorable Figures

In the Browns' 60 years of existence, including the three years the franchise was dormant after Art Modell's move to Baltimore, the team has boasted thousands of talented football players, hundreds of stars, and more than a few dozen genuine characters.

Here is an alphabetical list of 21 memorable figures in the history of the franchise who have not been profiled elsewhere in this book. It's subjective and is not meant to be a list of the best players or the most important figures, although some of those certainly are included. Undoubtedly some fan favorites have been left out. That's just the nature of such a discussion.

Abe Abraham, aka "The Man in the Brown Suit" (1946–82). Most fans never knew Abraham's name—they only knew he was the guy who caught field goals and punts behind the west end zone. According to the Browns, Abraham was a part-time employee stationed at the pass gate at the old Cleveland Municipal Stadium back in 1946. One day he had to deliver a message to a doctor, and as he made his way across the west end of the field, a field goal kicked by Lou Groza sailed through the uprights. Abraham fielded the ball, but the force of the kick knocked him down and he suffered bruised ribs. He got such a reaction from the fans, however, that he returned to catch another kick later in the game—and continued to do so until his death in 1982 at the age of 74. A campaign to get him into the Pro Football Hall of Fame finally succeeded in 2001, when he was inducted into the Visa Hall of Fans.

Tackle **Orlando Brown** (1994–95, 1999). At 6'7" and 375 pounds, Brown, nicknamed "Zeus," stands tall as the Browns' biggest player ever. The South Carolina State product played two seasons with the team before the move to Baltimore, and then he got a $27-million deal—the

TRIVIA

Who scored the first rushing touchdown for the new Browns in Cleveland Browns Stadium in 1999?

Answers to the trivia questions are on pages 159–160.

largest ever for an offensive lineman—to come back and provide some leadership on the new Browns team. Unfortunately, things didn't work out as planned. On December 19 referee Jeff Triplette accidentally hit Brown in the right eye with a penalty flag. (The flags are weighted with three ounces of metal BBs.) Brown covered his eye with his hands and fell to one knee as teammates rushed to his side and helped him to the sideline. But he stormed back onto the field, shoved Triplette to the ground, and stood over him screaming. Teammates again led him away. He was ejected from that game and eventually suspended by the league for two more. He spent six days in the hospital. Some time later Brown revealed that his father had glaucoma and was blind, a fact that undoubtedly had something to do with his outburst. He sued the NFL for $200 million, settled for a reported $10 million, and returned to play for the Baltimore Ravens.

Quarterback **Tim Couch** (1999–2003). The Kentucky quarterback, taken with the number one overall pick in the 1999 draft, was supposed to become the face of the new franchise and lead the Browns back to glory. Things didn't quite work out that way. In fact, it seemed as if the Browns started questioning Couch's abilities shortly after they decided to make him the number one pick, bypassing players like Central Florida quarterback Daunte Culpepper, Syracuse quarterback Donovan McNabb, Texas running back Ricky Williams, and Oregon quarterback Akili Smith. Couch, who grew up in the tiny coal mining town of Hyden, Kentucky, had skills and size at 6'4", 227 pounds. He was Kentucky's Mr. Football at Leslie County High School. He set every passing record at the University of Kentucky, along with some conference and national records. He completed 72 percent of his passes as a junior, 67 percent for his career, and had 73 touchdowns with only 34 interceptions during his last two seasons. He skipped his senior year to turn pro and, after professing his love for the Browns, seemed like a natural fit, especially with new coach Chris Palmer, who was known for his work with young quarterbacks.

As a rookie Couch was expecting to be brought along gradually behind former BYU Heisman Trophy winner Ty Detmer. But Detmer was injured and Couch took over in the second game of the season, ready or not. As with any expansion team and any young player, there were highs and lows. But behind the scenes, football observers started questioning Couch's arm strength and leadership qualities. That led to perpetual quarterback controversies. Some think Couch never quite recovered in the public eye after a concussion in a 2002 game against the Baltimore Ravens that led to a teary outburst against the fans who cheered while he was down. Couch made it through the 2003 season before being released in 2004.

Kicker **Phil Dawson** (1999–present). If the new Browns got one thing right, it was signing free agent Dawson on March 25, 1999; he now holds the longest tenure of any player on the expansion team. A former All-American at the University of Texas, Dawson was not taken in the draft; instead he signed with the Oakland Raiders in 1998 and then was

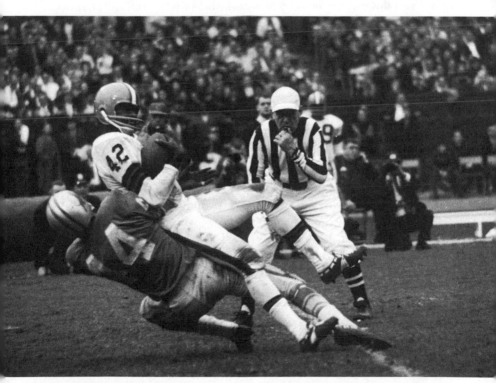

Paul Warfield (No. 42) is one of 15 Browns in the Hall of Fame. Photo courtesy of Diamond Images.

released. He was claimed off waivers by the New England Patriots and spent the 1998 season on the practice squad. In seven seasons with the Browns he has seven game-winning kicks, including three that came on the last play of the game.

Guard **Joe DeLamielleure** (1980–84). DeLamielleure made a name for himself in Buffalo from 1973 to 1979, where he was part of the offensive line that cleared the way for O. J. Simpson. He made the Pro Bowl five years in a row and was named the American Football Conference Lineman of the Year in 1975. He was traded to Cleveland for two second-round picks during a contract dispute in 1980 and promptly made the Pro Bowl again. He spent five seasons with the Browns and played with the Kardiac Kids in 1980 before returning to Buffalo for the 1985 season. He was one of a kind. In *Tales from the Browns Sidelines* by Tony Grossi, DeLamielleure revealed that he wore apple slices in his socks because he'd met a doctor for the king of Saudi Arabia who told him holding fruit or vegetables to his body would make him stronger. He made the Pro Football Hall of Fame on his 13th try, which he figured was fitting because he signed his first contract on Friday the 13th, there were 13 letters in his last name, he played for 13 seasons, and the story came across the Associated Press wire at 3:13.

Cornerbacks **Hanford Dixon** (1981–89) and **Frank Minnifield** (1984–92). These two individuals were so closely identified with each other that it just makes sense to treat them as one entry here. In recent years they became so well known for promoting the Dawg Pound concept that their talents on the football field sometimes were forgotten—although that wasn't the case for the fans who saw them play or the opponents they faced. In fact, they were probably the greatest pair of defensive backs the Browns ever had, and they have to rank near the top in NFL history as well. Dixon was a first-round draft choice in 1981 from Southern Mississippi. Minnifield, who'd played college football at Louisville, came over from the USFL in 1984. They became the first pair of cornerbacks from the same team to start in the Pro Bowl in 1987, and they did it again in 1988. They were years ahead of their time when it came to using computers to log information on their foes as a part of preparation for games.

Defensive end **Len Ford** (1950–57). Ford started his career with the Los Angeles Dons in the All-America Football Conference, where he played offense and defense, catching 67 passes as a rookie in 1948 and

IF ONLY . . . Jerry Sherk had not developed a life-threatening staph infection in 1979 that prematurely ended his career, he surely would have been elected to the Pro Football Hall of Fame as one of the finest defensive tackles ever to play in the NFL.

1949. When the AAFC folded he joined the Browns, who used him exclusively on defense. A broken nose and cheekbone cut short his first season in Cleveland, but he recovered to become an All-NFL selection from 1951 to 1955, a four-time Pro Bowl player, and a 1976 enshrinee in the Pro Football Hall of Fame. He was a great pass rusher who liked to jump over linemen like the former basketball star he was. He even played with the legendary barnstorming New York Rens basketball team. He died of a heart attack on March 14, 1972, at the age of 46.

Center **Frank Gatski** (1946–56). All those passes Otto Graham threw, all those runs Marion Motley made, all those receptions Dante Lavelli pulled in—they all started when Gatski hiked the ball to the quarterback. His durability was amazing. He reportedly never missed a practice or game in high school in West Virginia, in college at Marshall, or in his 12-year pro career. He played in 11 championship games in 12 years, with his team winning eight titles. A four-time All-NFL selection, he played in the Pro Bowl in 1957 and was elected to the Pro Football Hall of Fame in 1985. He died on November 23, 2005, of congestive heart failure at the age of 83.

Running back **Ben Gay** (2001). Maybe it was the name, but for his one season with the Browns, Gay became a media darling and a fan favorite. He garnered much more publicity than one would have expected given his modest statistics: he had 51 carries for 172 yards and one touchdown; he caught four passes for 11 yards and had 23 kickoff returns for 513 yards. As his legend grew, *The Plain Dealer* investigated his background at Garden City Community College in Kansas. Gay told the newspaper that at one time he was a drunk who sold crack cocaine and heroin and shot at people in gang wars. His college coach, Bob Larsen, told the paper, "He's full of charm and charisma, but he'd rather tell a lie when the truth would do just fine." He was released after the Browns drafted running back William Green.

Nose tackle **Bob Golic** (1982–88). A Cleveland native, Golic played at St. Joseph High School and became an All-American linebacker at the

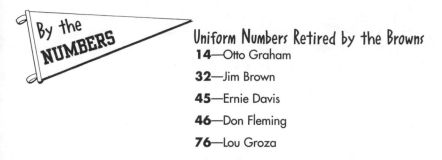

By the NUMBERS

Uniform Numbers Retired by the Browns

14—Otto Graham

32—Jim Brown

45—Ernie Davis

46—Don Fleming

76—Lou Groza

University of Notre Dame before being drafted by New England in the second round in 1979. He came to the Browns in 1982 and was switched from linebacker to nose tackle, playing well enough at the new position to be named to the Pro Bowl from 1985 to 1987. He finished his playing days with the Raiders in Los Angeles, where he started an acting career that included parts in sit-coms like *Coach* and *Saved by the Bell—The College Years*. But he missed sports, and since his retirement in 1992, he has worked in radio and television for NBC Sports, Fox Sports Net, CNN, and ESPN. In 2005 he worked on the Browns' preseason telecasts on Cleveland's WOIO, Channel 19.

Kick returner/running back **Dino Hall** (1979–83). Doug Dieken, a former Browns tackle and longtime broadcaster with the team, called Hall the toughest guy who ever played with the Browns. That's saying something for a guy who was 5'7" and 165 pounds. He came to the Browns as the NCAA Division III rushing leader from Glassboro State, but the team rarely used him at running back. Instead he excelled on special teams, leading the Browns in punt and kickoff returns three times each. In fact, in his first game he tied an NFL record with 172 yards on nine kickoff returns against Pittsburgh. He still holds team records for kick returns (151) and yards (3,185).

Linebacker **Eddie Johnson** (1981–90). A seventh-round draft choice from the University of Louisville in 1981, Johnson was nicknamed "The Assassin" because of his lethal approach on defense. But off the field he was involved in many community and charitable causes, including the Eddie Johnson Foundation. It's possible that he's the most beloved Browns player of all time. When he died at the age of 43 on January 21, 2003, after a 27-month battle with colon cancer, dozens of former teammates attended the memorial service. Johnny Davis played the keyboards and Cleo Miller sang the Lord's Prayer. He was eulogized by

Bernie Kosar, Earnest Byner, Dave Puzzuoli, Felix Wright, Dick Ambrose, Reggie Langhorne, Herman Fontenot, and Ricky Feacher.

Running back **Leroy Kelly** (1964–73). Filling the cleats of Hall of Fame running back Jim Brown was not an easy task, but Kelly proved to be more than up for it, making the Hall of Fame himself in 1994. In fact, in each of his first three seasons as the featured back, the eighth-round draft choice from Morgan State rushed for more than 1,000 yards, leading the league in rushing in 1967 and 1968. He also was a two-time punt-return champion, leading the NFL in 1965 and the AFC in 1971. His 12,329 combined yards (7,274 rushing, 2,281 receiving, and 2,774 returning) rank second only to Jim Brown in Browns history. He still holds the Browns' single-season record for punt-return average (15.59 yards in 1965).

Linebacker **Clay Matthews** (1978–93). The first-round draft choice from Southern Cal grew up around football. His father, Clay Sr., was a defensive end with San Francisco, and his brother Bruce was an All-Pro with the Houston Oilers. A smart player against the run or the pass, Matthews, who drove his Mercury Capri to training camp from California every year, played 16 seasons with the Browns and owns the club's NFL record for most games played with 232. Matthews was 40 when he retired from Atlanta in 1996.

Tackle **Mike McCormack** (1954–62). McCormack started his career with the New York Yanks in 1951 and then spent two years in the United States army before being traded to Cleveland in a 15-player deal. McCormack was linked to some of the greatest minds in football. He was coached by Pop Warner at Kansas, played for Paul Brown, and coached with Brown, Vince Lombardi, and George Allen. Brown presented him when McCormack went into the Pro Football Hall of Fame in 1984, calling him the finest offensive tackle in pro football.

Wide receiver/kick returner **Gerald "Ice Cube" McNeil** (1986–89). Dino Hall looked like a giant compared to McNeil, who was 5'7" and 140

DID YOU KNOW . . . That while the Browns' offense was much heralded in the early days, their defense against scoring was number one in all four years of the All-America Football Conference and in four of their first six years in the National Football League?

IF ONLY . . .

The new Browns had made Donovan McNabb their first quarterback, pairing him with former Syracuse teammate and wide receiver Kevin Johnson, the team would certainly have made more than one playoff appearance since its return in 1999.

pounds soaking wet. His nickname fit him perfectly, however, as he slipped and slid through tackles while leading the NFL in kickoff returns in 1986 and punt returns in 1989. He was the Browns' all-time leader with 161 punt returns and 1,545 yards until being overtaken by Dennis Northcutt in 2005. McNeil had a 100-yard kickoff return for a touchdown against Pittsburgh and an 84-yard punt return for a touchdown against Detroit (both in 1986). He also set single-season records with 49 returns for 496 yards in 1989.

Running back **Bobby Mitchell** (1958–61). A seventh-round draft choice from Illinois, Mitchell used his ability as a sprinter and hurdler to achieve long scoring runs. He was the perfect complement to roommate Jim Brown's steady power. Mitchell never resented the fact that Paul Brown traded him to the Washington Redskins in 1962, making him the first African American in that franchise's history. He played in Washington until 1968. In return the Browns got the rights to Ernie Davis, the Redskins' first-round draft choice from Syracuse, who died of leukemia in 1963, never playing for the Browns. When all was said and done Mitchell had 14,078 combined net yards, scored 91 touchdowns, caught 521 passes, and had eight kick returns for touchdowns. He still holds the Browns' career record for kickoff returns for touchdowns with three. He went into the Pro Football Hall of Fame in 1983.

Defensive tackle **Michael Dean Perry** (1988–94). His older brother, William "The Refrigerator" Perry, got all the attention while playing for the Chicago Bears. But Michael Dean Perry was a better player. A second-round draft choice in 1988 from Clemson, he started winning awards as a rookie and never stopped. He was an all-NFL selection in 1989, 1990, 1991, and 1994, and he played in the Pro Bowl in 1990, 1991, 1992, 1994, and 1995. His brother may have earned a Super Bowl ring, but Michael Dean's trophy case has more hardware.

Defensive tackle **Jerry Sherk** (1970–81). Some believe Sherk was the best defensive tackle the Browns ever had. In 1972 he was named the defensive player of the year by the Cleveland Touchdown Club. In 1974 and 1975 his teammates voted him the team's most valuable player, and in 1975 the league's offensive linemen voted him the league's defensive lineman of the year. In 1976 he was named the league's best defensive lineman. However, in 1977, he suffered a partially torn medial collateral ligament in his left knee and missed most of the season. He was back in form in 1979 and was leading the league with 12 sacks when he scraped his elbow on the turf at Veterans Stadium in Philadelphia, opening a boil that had developed there. A staph infection set in, settling in his left knee. He spent more than a month in the Cleveland Clinic, where doctors feared he might lose his leg or his life.

Wide receiver **Paul Warfield** (1964–69, 1976–77). In between his two stints with the Browns, Warfield spent five seasons with the Miami Dolphins after the Browns traded him for the third pick in the 1970 draft, which they used to take Mike Phipps. The former Ohio State star who grew up in Warren, Ohio, and attended Harding High School could do it all. He was fast and strong with exceptional hands. He ran great patterns and was a good blocker, too. His career stats included 427 passes for 8,565 yards and 85 touchdowns. With the Browns he had 5,210 yards (fourth on the Browns' career receiving list) and 52 touchdowns (second on the Browns' career list). He had 1,067 yards receiving in 1968, the third-best receiving season in Browns history. He was enshrined in the Pro Football Hall of Fame in 1983.

The Keeper of the Flame

The door to the Cleveland Browns' archives opens and a familiar smell wafts into the hallway.

It's the smell of old newspapers, a stale scent that evokes the sweet memory of a different era: reporters in fedoras, pecking away on type-writers; copy editors in green eyeshades, armed with thick yellow pencils; copy boys in knickers hawking newspapers on the corner.

The yellowed newspapers are bound in heavy brown files, stacked along walls and piled on tables. They're the oldest things in the new Cleveland Browns stadium.

Oh, there are old programs, too, and photographs and score sheets and statistics crammed into gray filing cabinets. There are film canisters and videotapes arranged by year on shelves. If it happened to the Cleveland Browns, there's a record of it in this room.

Dino Lucarelli is the keeper of the flame. As the Browns' manager of alumni relations, he is responsible for keeping the team's past up to date. His office is an extension of the archives, filled with mementoes of his more than 30 years with the team. Autographed pictures hang on the walls. Footballs in Plexiglas cases are lined up atop the cherry wood cabinets behind his desk. One whole wall is taken up with old press guides and all the books that have been written on the Browns. It's a one-wall library and a one-room shrine to greatness.

There's a colored print of Lou Groza, a black-and-white sketch of Doug Dieken talking to a referee (about a holding call, no doubt). There's a poster of the 1964 championship team, along with framed memos and proclamations. Right in the middle, seemingly out of place, is a huge picture of Vince Lombardi. It was a gift from the former Cleveland *Plain*

Dealer artist who drew it—Vince Matteucci. The "Vince" signature is his, not Lombardi's.

Lucarelli smiles as he lovingly recalls each item. He was 12 years old when the Cleveland Browns were born in 1946 as part of the All-America Football Conference. He remembers their first game—a 44–0 victory over the Miami Seahawks at Cleveland Municipal Stadium. He went to the game with his brother and sister-in-law. They owned a bar in Garfield Heights called Ceo's, and they had 50 season tickets. But a kid could get in for a quarter, so Lucarelli paid 25 cents and watched the game from under the old Longine's clock. He was wearing a bright red corduroy shirt so his brother and sister-in-law could keep an eye on him with their binoculars.

Thus began a 60-year relationship that has only grown deeper throughout the years. "I'm a happy camper," said Lucarelli, who is often confused with Browns Hall of Fame receiver Dante Lavelli because of the similarity of their last names.

Lucarelli grew up on Grand Division Street on the southeast side of Cleveland. One side of the street was in Cleveland, while the other was in Garfield Heights. Lucarelli was a football fan, but he never played organized football, although he did play organized baseball and basketball. He attended Garfield Heights High School and went to night school at Fenn College, which became Cleveland State University.

His work with the Cleveland media spans 50 years and includes stints with the semipro Cleveland Bulldogs football team, the original AHL Cleveland Barons, and then the Indians, where he worked in public relations, promotions, and sales. In those days the Indians and Browns shared a lunchroom at the old Cleveland Municipal Stadium, so all their employees knew each other. "Art Modell used to tell me all the time he wanted me to work for him someday," Lucarelli said.

By the
NUMBERS

Cleveland Browns Legends

34—Number of Cleveland Browns determined to be legends by a panel of voters and fans voting on Cleveland.com.

Inaugural Class: Jim Brown, Paul Brown, Len Ford, Frank Gatski, Otto Graham, Lou Groza, Leroy Kelly, Dante Lavelli, Mike McCormack, Bobby Mitchell, Marion Motley, Ozzie Newsome, Paul Warfield, and Bill Willis. Joe DeLamielleure was added after his enshrinement in the Pro Football Hall of Fame in 2003.

Class of 2001: Ray Renfro, Gene Hickerson, Greg Pruitt, Bernie Kosar, and Michael Dean Perry.

Class of 2002: Mac Speedie, Brian Sipe, and Clay Matthews.

Class of 2003: Bob Gain, Dick Schafrath, and Hanford Dixon.

Class of 2004: Tommy James, Dub Jones, Gary Collins, and Mike Pruitt.

Class of 2005: Jim Ray Smith, Frank Ryan, Jerry Sherk, and Frank Minnifield.

Someday arrived in 1975. Although Lucarelli was originally hired to work in public relations for the Cleveland Stadium Corporation, slowly but surely he became more involved with the Browns. He has become such a fixture that when the Browns opened their new media center at their Berea headquarters, they named it after Lucarelli. "One of the biggest thrills of my life," Lucarelli admits.

But most of the tireless work he does is behind the scenes—whether it's filling in a reporter from Albuquerque on the details of Red Right 88 or persuading Hall of Famer Bill Willis to do yet another interview for yet another book on the history of the Browns. Generally speaking, former players find it tough to say no to him.

"I don't know if it's the Father Flanagan in him, but Dino is such a good person," Hall of Famer Ozzie Newsome said. "He never used his job to gain anything personal. He would do anything and everything for you. Dino is one of the great people in this world, as far as I'm concerned."

Added broadcaster and former offensive lineman Dieken, "They don't get any better. He is the best—a super, super guy. Everybody who knows Dino loves him. He's one of the finest persons you could find."

As part of his position, Lucarelli works to keep tabs on all the former players and serves as a liaison between them and the current organization. He's responsible for the team's frequent reunions, and he's also in charge of facilitating interviews between former players and authors or reporters.

Although he's much too nice to complain about it, it upsets him when he hears people say the Browns don't care about their alumni. "This team is so alumni conscious, but ironically, we're not perceived that way," he said. "I read something recently where former Cavalier Campy Russell said the Browns and Indians have such good alumni programs, and I was thrilled. We had a player, Ron Johnson, a number one draft choice in 1969. He only played for us for one year, but he played for the New York Giants eight or nine years. He told somebody he never hears from the Giants, but he always hears from us. That made me feel good."

Lucarelli and assistant Geri Pastor constantly try to improve the team's alumni relations. They produce a newsletter, coordinate all

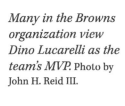

Many in the Browns organization view Dino Lucarelli as the team's MVP. Photo by John H. Reid III.

alumni functions, and are responsible for the distribution of game tickets to former players. In addition, intern Erika Mason has spent months using a computer to photograph all those fragile old newspapers so researching the history of the Browns will be easier. It's as if Lucarelli wants everyone to know as much about the team as he does.

"I love what I'm doing," he said. "It's the best job I ever had. It keeps me in contact with our history."

ANSWERS TO TRIVIA QUESTIONS

Page 3: Cliff Lee of Lakewood, Ohio, and Duke University started at quarterback for the Browns in their first AAFC game. Otto Graham was late to training camp because he was playing for the College All-Star team that beat the Los Angeles Rams 16–0 on August 23, 1946.

Page 14: In addition to No. 14, Otto Graham also wore No. 60. He played safety in addition to quarterback.

Page 19: Bill Willis's middle name is Karnet.

Page 23: Horace Gillom holds the record for the longest punt in Browns history—80 yards—kicked in a game against the New York Giants on November 28, 1954.

Page 29: The 11 future Hall of Famers on the field for the 1950 championship game were Len Ford, Frank Gatski, Otto Graham, Lou Groza, Dante Lavelli, Marion Motley, and Bill Willis for the Browns and Tom Fears, Elroy "Crazy Legs" Hirsch, Norm Van Brocklin, and Bob Waterfield for the Rams.

Page 40: The two numbers worn by Lou Groza while with the Browns were No. 76, which was retired by the team, and No. 46.

Page 46: The two passes not thrown by Graham or Ratterman in 1955 were thrown by wide receiver Ray Renfro, who also filled in on defense. Renfro threw two passes but failed to complete either.

Page 51: The five sports Jim Brown played in high school were football, basketball, baseball, track, and lacrosse.

Page 68: The announcers for ABC's first *Monday Night Football* broadcast were Howard Cosell, Keith Jackson, and Don Meredith.

Page 77: Lou Saban, the AFL Coach of the Year with Buffalo in 1964 and 1965, gave Sam Rutigliano his first job in pro football. Saban asked Rutigliano to accompany him from the University of Maryland to the Denver Broncos for the 1967 season. Saban was the head coach at Maryland at the time, and Rutigliano was an assistant.

Page 85: Before attending San Diego State, Brian Sipe attended Grossmont College in El Cajon, California.

Page 88: Besides Ozzie Newsome, USC linebacker Clay Matthews was the Browns' other first-round draft choice in 1978.

Page 108: Only four penalties were committed during the 1986 AFC Championship game—just one by the Browns and three by the Broncos in a game that was remarkably clean.

Page 119: The first two pairs of running backs to rush for 1,000 yards in one season were Miami's Larry Csonka and Mercury Morris in 1972 and Pittsburgh's Franco Harris and Rocky Bleier in 1976.

Page 125: Bernie Kosar earned his University of Miami degrees in finance and economics.

Page 131: The city of Baltimore approached the Cincinnati Bengals before reaching a deal with Cleveland owner Art Modell.

Page 134: The first players obtained by Carmen Policy for the new Browns were tight end Irv Smith and defensive end Roy Barker from the San Francisco 49ers, in return for past considerations, on February 12, 1999.

Page 143: From their inception into the All-America Football Conference in 1946 through 2005, the Browns have missed the playoffs 29 times, with 11 of those seasons coming since 1990. (This does not include 1996 to 1998, the three years the team was inactive.)

Page 146: On October 10, 1999, kicker Phil Dawson scored the first rushing touchdown for the new Browns in Cleveland Browns Stadium on a four-yard run after a fake field-goal attempt against Cincinnati.

Cleveland Browns
All-Time Roster
(through 2005 season)

* Denotes replacement player during 1987 players' strike.

# Denotes player on active roster who did not play in a game.

Denotes player on practice squad who did not play in a game.

Denotes player on injured reserve.

@ Denotes player on reserve with a nonfootball injury.

A

Abdul-Jabbar, Karim (RB) UCLA	1999
Abdullah, Rahim (LB) Clemson	1999–2000
Abrams, Bobby (LB) Michigan	1992
Adamle, Tony (LB) Ohio State	1947–51, 1954
Adams, Chet (T) Ohio University	1946–48
Adams, Pete (G) Southern California	1974, 1976
Adams, Stefon (DB) Auburn	1990
Adams, Vashone (DB) Eastern Michigan	1995
Adams, Willis (WR) Houston	1979–85
Aeilts, Rick (TE) Southeast Missouri State	##1989
Agase, Alex (G) Illinois	1948–51
Akins, Al (RB) Washington State	1946
Akins, Chris (DB) Arkansas–Pine Bluff	2001–02
Aldridge, Allen (DE) Prairie View	1974
Alexander, Derrick (WR) Michigan	1994–95
Alexander, Derrick (DL) Florida State	1999
Allamon, Kyle (TE) Texas Tech	##2000
Allen, Ermal (QB) Kentucky	1947
Allen, Greg (RB) Florida State	1985
Alston, Richard (WR) East Carolina	2004

Alzado, Lyle (DE) Yankton	1979–81
Ambrose, Dick (LB) Virginia	1975–83
Amstutz, Joe (C) Indiana	1957
Anderson, Derek (QB) Oregon State	#2005
Anderson, Herbie (DB) Texas A&I	##1992
Anderson, Preston (DB) Rice	1974
Anderson, Stuart (LB) Virginia	1984
Andrew, Troy (OL) Duke	##2003
Andrews, Billy (LB) Southeastern Louisiana	1967–74
Andruzzi, Joe (G) S. Connecticut State	2005
Arvie, Herman (OL) Grambling	1993–95
Askin, John (G) Notre Dame	*1987
Athas, Pete (DB) Tennessee	1975
Atkins, Doug (DE) Tennessee	1953–54

B

Baab, Mike (C) Texas	1982–87, 1990–91
Babich, Bob (LB) Miami (Ohio)	1973–78
Bahr, Matt (K) Penn State	1981–89
Baker, Al (DE) Colorado State	1987, 1989–90
Baker, Sam (P, K) Oregon State	1960–61
Baker, Tony (RB) East Carolina	1986, 1988
Baldwin, Keith (DE) Texas A&M	1982–85
Baldwin, Randy (RB) Mississippi	#1991–94
Ball, Jerry (DT) Southern Methodist	1993, 1999
Bandison, Romeo (DL) Oregon	#1994–95
Banker, Ted (G) Southeast Mississippi State	1989
Banks, Carl (LB) Michigan State	1994–95
Banks, Chip (LB) Southern California	1982–86
Banks, Fred (WR) Liberty	1985

Banks, Robert (DE) Notre Dame	1989–90	
Barisich, Carl (DT) Princeton	1973–75	
Barker, Roy (DE) North Carolina	1999	
Barnes, Erich (DB) Purdue	1965–71	
Barnes, Rashidi (DB) Colorado	2000	
Barnett, Harlon (S) Michigan State	1990–92	
Barnett, Vincent (S) Arkansas State	*1987	
Barney, Eppie (WR) Iowa State	1967–68	
Bassett, Maurice (RB) Langston	1954–56	
Bates, Michael (WR, KR) Arizona	1995	
Battle, Jim (DE) Southern University	1966	
Baugh, Tom (C) Southern Illinois	1989	
Bavaro, Mark (TE) Notre Dame	1992	
Baxter, Gary (DB) Baylor	2005	
Beach, Walter (DB) Central Michigan	1963–66	
Beamon, Autry (DB) East Texas State	1980–81	
Beasley, Chad (OT) Virginia Tech	2002–03	
Beauford, Clayton (WR) Auburn	*1987	
Bedell, Brad (OL) Colorado	2000–01	
Bedosky, Mike (OL) Missouri	#1994	
Belk, Rocky (WR) Miami	1983	
Bell, Geno (DL) Arkansas	##1999	
Bell, Shonn (TE) Virginia-Wise	##2001	
Bell, Terry (WR) Indiana State	*1987	
Bentley, Kevin (LB) Northwestern	2002–04	
Benz, Larry (DB) Northwestern	1963–65	
Bernstein, Alex (OL) Amherst	#1999	
Berry, Latin (DB) Oregon	1991–92	
Best, Greg (S) Kansas State	1984	
Bettridge, Ed (LB) Bowling Green	1964	
Beutler, Tom (LB) Toledo	1970	
Biedermann, Leo (T) California	1978	
Bingham, Tramaine (DE) Ouachita Baptist	##2002	
Bishop, Harold (TE) Louisiana State	1995	
Black, James (RB) Akron	1984	
Blanchard, Billy (RB) Murray State	##2003	
Blandin, Ernie (T) Tulane	1946–47	
Blaylock, Anthony (DB) Winston-Salem	1988–91	
Bloch, Ray (T) Ohio University	#1981	
Bobo, Orlando (G) Northeast Louisiana	1999	
Bodden, Leigh (DB) Duquesne	2003–05	

Boedeker, Bill (RB) No College	1947–49	
Bolden, Leroy (RB) Michigan State	1958–59	
Bolden, Rickey (T) Southern Methodist	1984–89	
Bolton, Ron (DB) Norfolk State	1976–82	
Bolzan, Scott (T) Northern Illinois	#1985	
Booth, Issac (DB) California	1994–95	
Booty, Josh (QB) Louisiana State	#2001–03	
Borton, John (QB) Ohio State	1957	
Borum, Jarvis (OL) North Carolina State	##2002	
Bosley, Keith (OT) Eastern Kentucky	*1987	
Bostic, Keith (DB) Michigan	1990	
Bowers, R. J. (FB) Grove City (Pennsylvania)	2002–03	
Boyer, Brant (LB) Arizona	2001–03	
Bradley, Harold (G) Iowa	1954–56	
Bradley, Henry (DT) Alcorn State	1979–82	
Brady, Donny (DB) Wisconsin	1995	
Braggs, Stephen (DB) Texas	1987–91	
Brandon, David (LB) Memphis State	1991–93	
Brannon, Robert (DE) Arkansas	*1987	
Braziel, Larry (CB) Southern California	1982–85	
Brennan, Brian (WR) Boston College	1984–91	
Brewer, Johnny (TE, LB) Mississippi	1961–67	
Brewster, Darrel (WR) Purdue	1952–58	
Briggs, Bob (DE) Heidelberg	1971–73	
Briggs, Greg (S) Texas Southern	##1993	
Briggs, Kris (FB) Southern Methodist	##2004	
Brinkman, Charles (WR) Louisville	1972	
Brockman, Lonnie (LB) West Virginia	##1991	
Brohm, Jeff (QB) Louisville	#2000	
Brooks, Clifford (DB) Tennessee State	1972–74	
Brooks, James (RB) Auburn	1992	
Brown, Bobby (WR) Notre Dame	2000, ##2001	
Brown, Courtney (DE) Penn State	2000–04	
Brown, Dante (RB) Memphis	##2004	
Brown, Dean (DB) Fort Valley State	1969	
Brown, Dee (RB) Syracuse	2004	
Brown, Eddie (DB) Tennessee	1974–75	
Brown, James (OL) Virginia State	2000	
Brown, Jerome (DL) Mississippi State	##1993	
Brown, Jim (RB) Syracuse	1957–65	
Brown, John (T) Syracuse	1962–66	

Brown, John III (WR) Houston	##1992	Carraway, Stanley (WR) West Texas State	*1987
Brown, Ken (RB) No College	1970–75	Carreker, Vince (DB) Cincinnati	*1987
Brown, Lomas (T) Florida	1999	Carrier, Mark (WR) Nicholls State	1993–94
Brown, Marvin (FB) Alabama	##2002	Carter, Alex (DE) Tennessee State	*1987
Brown, Orlando (T) South Carolina State	1994–95, 1999	Carter, Dyshod (DB) Kansas State	2001, 2004
		Carver, Dale (LB) Georgia	1983
Brown, Preston (KR) Vanderbilt	1984	Cassady, Howard (RB) Ohio State	1962
Brown, Richard (LB) San Diego State	1991–92	Catlin, Tom (LB) Oklahoma	1953–54, 1957–58
Brown, Stan (WR) Purdue	1971	Caylor, Lowell (DB) Miami (Ohio)	1964
Brown, Terry (DB) Oklahoma State	1976	Chambers, Kirk (OL) Stanford	2004–05
Brown, Thomas (DE) Baylor	1981, 1983	Chanoine, Roger (OL) Temple	1999–2002
Bryant, Antonio (WR) Pittsburgh	2004–05	Chapman, Lamar (DB) Kansas State	2000–01
Buben, Mark (DT) Tufts	1982	Charlton, Clifford (LB) Florida	1988–89
Buchanan, Charles (DE) Tennessee State	1988	Cheroke, George (G) Ohio State	1946
Buczkowski, Bob (DL) Pittsburgh	1990	Chiaverini, Darrin (WR) Colorado	1999–2000
Buddenberg, John (OL) Akron	##1989	Childress, Freddie (T) Arkansas	1992
Buehler, George (G) Stanford	1978–79	Christensen, Jeff (QB) Eastern Illinois	*1987
Bumgardner, Rex (RB) West Virginia	1950–52	Clancy, Sam (DE) Pittsburgh	1985–88
Bundra, Mike (DT) Southern California	1964	Clark, Monte (T) Southern California	1963–69
Bundren, Jim (C) Clemson	1999–2000	Clarke, Frank (WR) Colorado	1957–59
Burnett, Chester (LB) Arizona	2000	Clarke, Leon (WR) Southern California	1960–62
Burnett, Rob (DE) Syracuse	1990–95	Claxton, Ben (OL) Mississippi	##2003
Burrell, Clinton (DB) Louisiana State	1979–84	Clayborn, Raymond (CB) Texas	1990–91
Burton, Leonard (OL) South Carolina	#1991	Claybrooks, DeVone (DL) East Carolina	2001
Bush, Devin (DB) Florida State	2001–02	Claybrooks, Felipe (DL) Georgia Tech	2001–03, ##2004
Butler, Dave (LB) Notre Dame	*1987	Clemons, Chris (LB) Georgia	##2001
Butler, Ray (WR) Southern California	#1989	Cline, Ollie (RB) Ohio State	1948
Byner, Earnest (RB) East Carolina	1984–88, 1994–95	Coates, Sherrod (LB) Western Kentucky	2003–04
		Cockroft, Don (K, P) Adams State	1968–80
C		Cole, Emerson (RB) Toledo	1950–52
Caldwell, Mike (LB) Middle Tennessee State	1993–95	Colella, Tom (P, DB) Canisius	1946–48
Caleb, Jamie (RB) Grambling	1960, 1965	Coleman, Cosey (G) Tennessee	2005
Camp, Reggie (DE) California	1983–87	Coleman, Greg (P) Florida A&M	1977
Campbell, Mark (TE) Michigan	1999–2002	Colinet, Stalin (DL) Boston College	1999–2001
Campbell, Milt (RB) Indiana	1957	Collins, Gary (WR, P) Maryland	1962–71
Capers, James (LB) Central Michigan	*1987	Collins, Javiar (OL) Northwestern	#2004
Carollo, Joe (T) Notre Dame	1972–73	Collins, Larry (RB) Texas A&I	1978
Carpenter, Chad (WR) Washington State	##1999	Collins, Ryan (TE) St. Thomas	#1999
Carpenter, Ken (RB) Oregon State	1950–53	Collins, Shawn (WR) Northern Arizona	1992
Carpenter, Lew (RB) Arkansas	1957–58	Colman, Doug (LB) Nebraska	2000
Carpenter, Preston (RB) Arkansas	1956–59	Colo, Don (T) Brown	1953–58

Conjar, Larry (RB) Notre Dame	1967
Connolly, Ted (G) Tulsa	1963
Conover, Frank (DL) Syracuse	1991
Contz, Bill (T) Penn State	1983–86
Conway, Brett (K) Penn State	2003
Cook, Damion (OL) Bethune-Cookman	2004
Cooks, Johnie (LB) Mississippi State	1991
Cooper, Deke (DB) Notre Dame	##2001
Cooper, Scott (DE) Kearney State	*1987
Copeland, Jim (G) Virginia	1967–74
Coppage, Alton (DE) Oklahoma	1946
Cornell, Bo (RB) Washington	1971–72
Costello, Vince (LB) Ohio University	1957–66
Cotton, Fest (DT) Dayton	1972
Cotton, Marcus (LB) Southern California	1990
Couch, Tim (QB) Kentucky	1999–2003
Cousineau, Tom (LB) Ohio State	1982–85
Cowan, Bob (RB) Indiana	1947–48
Cowher, Bill (LB) North Carolina State	1980–82
Cox, Arthur (TE) Texas South	1991
Cox, Steve (P, K) Arkansas	1981–84
Craig, Neal (DB) Fisk	1975–76
Craig, Reggie (WR) Arkansas	1977
Craven, Bill (DB) Harvard	1976
Crawford, Mike (RB) Arizona State	*1987
Crawford, Tim (LB) Texas Tech	*1987
Crespino, Bob (WR) Mississippi	1961–63
Crews, Ron (DE) Nevada–Las Vegas	1980
Cribbs, Josh (WR) Kent State	2005
Crocker, Chris (DB) Marshall	2003–05
Crosby, Cleveland (DE) Arizona	#1980
Cureton, Will (QB) East Texas State	1975
Cvercko, Andy (G) Northwestern	1963

D

Dahl, Bob (OL) Notre Dame	1992–95
Daniell, Jim (C) Ohio State	1946
Danielson, Gary (QB) Purdue	1985, 1987–88
Darden, Thom (DB) Michigan	1972–74, 1976–81
Dark, Steve (TE) Middle Tennessee State	##1993
Darrow, Barry (T) Montana	1974–78

Davis, Andra (LB) Florida	2002–05
Davis, André (WR) Virginia Tech	2002–04
Davis, Ben (DB) Defiance	1967–68, 1970–73
Davis, Bruce (WR) Baylor	1984
Davis, Dick (RB) Nebraska	1969
Davis, Gary (RB) Cal Poly–SLO	#1981
Davis, Johnny (RB) Alabama	1982–86, *1987
Davis, Michael (CB) Cincinnati	1995
Davis, Oliver (DB) Tennessee State	1977–80
Davis, Willie (DE) Grambling	1958–59
Davis, Zola (WR) South Carolina	1999
Dawson, Doug (G) Texas	1994
Dawson, JaJuan (WR) Tulane	2000–01
Dawson, Len (QB) Purdue	1960–61
Dawson, Lewis (OL) The Citadel	##2004–05
Dawson, Phil (K) Texas	1999–2005
Dearth, James (TE) Tarleton State	1999
DeLamielleure, Joe (G) Michigan State	1980–84
DeLeone, Tom (C) Ohio State	1974–84
DeLeone, Tony (P) Kent State	*1987
Dellerba, Spiro (RB) Ohio State	1947
DeMar, Enoch (OL) Indiana	2003–04
DeMarco, Bob (C) Dayton	1972–74
Demarie, John (G, T) Louisiana State	1967–75
Denman, Anthony (LB) Notre Dame	2001
Dennis, Al (G) Grambling	1976–77
Dennison, Doug (RB) Kutztown State	1979
Denton, Bob (DT) College of Pacific	1960
Deschaine, Dick (DE) No College	1958
Detmer, Ty (QB) Brigham Young	1999
Devries, Jed (OL) Utah State	##1994, 1995
Devrow, Billy (DB) Southern Mississippi	1967
Dewar, Jim (RB) Indiana	1947
Dickey, Curtis (RB) Texas A&M	1985–86
Dieken, Doug (T) Illinois	1971–84
Dilfer, Trent (QB) Fresno State	2005
Dimler, Rich (DT) Southern California	1979
Dixon, Gerald (LB) South Carolina	1993–95
Dixon, Hanford (CB) Southern Mississippi	1981–89
Donaldson, Gene (G) Kentucky	1953
Dorsey, Nat (OL) Georgia Tech	2005

Douglas, Derrick (RB) Louisiana Tech	1991	**F**	
Dressel, Chris (TE) Stanford	#1988	Faine, Jeff (C) Notre Dame	2003–05
Driver, Stacey (RB) Clemson	*1987	Fair, Carl (RB) Alabama-Birmingham	2001
Droughns, Reuben (RB) Oregon	2005	Fairchild, Greg (G) Tulsa	1978
Dudley, Brian (S) Bethune-Cookman	*1987	Farren, Paul (T) Boston University	1983–91
Dudley, Rickey (TE) Ohio State	2001	Feacher, Ricky (WR) Mississippi Valley	1976–84
Duff, Bill (DL) Tennessee	1999	Fekete, Gene (RB) Ohio State	1946
Dumont, Jim (LB) Rutgers	1984	Ferguson, Charley (DE) Tennessee A&I	1961
Dunbar, Jubilee (WR) Southern	1974	Ferguson, Vagas (RB) Notre Dame	1983
Duncan, Brian (RB) Southern Methodist	1976–77	Ferrell, Kerry (WR) Syracuse	##1993
Duncan, Ron (TE) Wittenberg	1967	Fichtner, Ross (DB) Purdue	1960–67
Dunn, Damon (WR) Stanford	1999–2000	Figaro, Cedric (LB) Notre Dame	1991–92
Dunn, David (WR) Fresno State	1999	Fike, Dan (G) Florida	1985–92
Dunn, Jonathan (T) Virginia Tech	###2005	Fisk, Jason (NT) Stanford	2005
Dutton, Ryan (P) Minnesota State–Mankato	#2004	Fiss, Galen (LB) Kansas	1956–66
Dyra, Jeff (DL) Northwestern	##2000	Fleming, Don (DB) Florida	1960–62
		Flick, Tom (QB) Washington	1984
E		Flint, Judson (DB) Memphis State	1980–82
Eason, Nick (DL) Clemson	2004–05	Florence, Anthony (DB) Bethune-Cookman	1991
East, Ron (DE) Montana State	1975	Floyd, Chris (FB) Michigan	2000
Eaton, Chad (DL) Washington State	#1995	Foggie, Fred (DB) Minnesota	1992
Echemandu, Adimchinobe (RB) California	2004	Fontenot, Herman (RB) Louisiana State	1985–88
Echols, Donnie (TE) Oklahoma State	*1987	Footman, Dan (DE) Florida State	1993–95
Edwards, Braylon (WR) Michigan	2005	Forbes, Marlon (S) Penn State	1999
Edwards, Earl (DT) Wichita State	1976–78	Ford, Henry (RB) Pittsburgh	1955
Edwards, Marc (FB) Notre Dame	1999–2000	Ford, Len (DE) Michigan	1950–57
Eitzmann, Chris (TE) Harvard	##2001	Forester, Herschel (G) Southern Methodist	1954–57
Ekuban, Ebenezer (DE) North Carolina	2004	Fortune, Elliott (DL) Georgia Tech	#1995
Elkins, Mike (QB) Wake Forest	#1991	Fowler, Melvin (C) Maryland	2002–04
Ellis, Ken (DB) Southern	1977	Francis, Jeff (QB) Tennessee	1990, #1992
Ellis, Ray (S) Ohio State	1986–87	Franco, Brian (K) Penn State	*1987
Ellsworth, Percy (DB) Virginia	2000–01	Franklin, Bobby (DB) Mississippi	1960–66
Engel, Steve (RB) Colorado	1970	Franks, Elvis (DE) Morgan State	1980–84
Estes, Steve (OL) Colgate	##2000	Franz, Todd (DB) Tulsa	2000
Ethridge, Ray (WR) Pasadena City	#1995	Fraser, Simon (DL) Ohio State	2005
Evans, Fred (RB) Notre Dame	1946	Frederick, Andy (T) New Mexico	1982
Evans, Johnny (QB, P) North Carolina State	1978–80	Frederick, Mike (DE) Virginia	1995
Everett, Major (RB) Mississippi College	1986, *1987	Freeman, Bob (QB) Auburn	1957–58
		Frost, Derrick (P) Northern Iowa	2003–04
Everitt, Steve (C) Michigan	1993–95	Frost, Scott (DB) Nebraska	2001
		Frye, Charlie (QB) Akron	2005

Fuller, Corey (DB) Florida State	1999–2002
Fullwood, Brent (RB) Auburn	1990
Fulton, Dan (WR) Nebraska-Omaha	1981–82
Furman, John (QB) Texas–El Paso	1962

G

Gain, Bob (DT) Kentucky	1952, 1954–64
Gainer, Derrick (RB) Florida A&M	##1989, 1990
Galbraith, Scott (TE) UCLA	1990–92
Garay, Antonio (DL) Boston College	2003
Garcia, Jeff (QB) San Jose State	2004
Garcia, Jim (DE) Purdue	1965
Gardner, Barry (LB) Northwestern	2003–04
Gardocki, Chris (P) Clemson	1999–2003
Garlington, John (LB) Louisiana State	1968–77
Garmon, Kelvin (OL) Baylor	2004
Gartner, Chris (K) Indiana	1974
Gash, Thane (S) East Tennessee State	1988–90
Gatski, Frank (C) Marshall	1946–56
Gaudio, Bob (G) Ohio State	1947–49, 1951
Gault, Don (QB) Hofstra	1970
Gautt, Prentice (RB) Oklahoma	1960
Gay, Benjamin (RB) Garden City Community College	2001
George, Tim (WR) Carson-Newman	1974
German, Jammi (WR) Miami (Florida)	2001
Gibron, Abe (G) Purdue	1950–56
Gibson, Damon (WR) Iowa	1999
Gibson, Tom (DE) Northern Arizona	1989–90
Gillom, Horace (P, WR) Nevada	1947–56
Gilmore, Corey (RB) San Diego State	*1987
Glass, Bill (DE) Baylor	1962–68
Glass, Chip (TE) Florida State	1969–73
Goad, Tim (DT) North Carolina	1995
Goebel, Brad (QB) Baylor	1992–94
Goins, Robert (S) Grambling	*1987
Golic, Bob (DT) Notre Dame	1982–88
Gonzalez, Joaquin (OT) Miami (Florida)	2002–04
Goode, Don (LB) Kansas	1980–81
Goosby, Tom (LB) Baldwin Wallace	1963
Gordon, Amon (DL) Stanford	2004–###05

Gorgal, Ken (DB) Purdue	1950, 1953–54
Goss, Don (DT) Southern Methodist	1956
Gossett, Jeff (P) Eastern Illinois	1983, 1985–87
Graf, Dave (LB) Penn State	1975–79
Graham, Earnest (RB) Florida	##2003
Graham, Jeff (QB) Long Beach State	##1989
Graham, Otto (QB) Northwestern	1946–55
Grant, Orantes (LB) Georgia	2003
Grant, Wes (DE) UCLA	1972
Graybill, Mike (OL) Boston University	1989
Grayson, David (LB) Fresno State	*1987–90
Graziani, Tony (QB) Oregon	#2000
Green, Boyce (RB) Carson-Newman	1983–85
Green, David (RB) Edinboro State	1982
Green, Ernie (RB) Louisville	1962–68
Green, Ron (WR) North Dakota	1967–68
Green, Van (DB) Shaw	1973–76
Green, William (RB) Boston College	2002–05
Greenwood, Don (RB) Illinois	1946–47
Greer, Terry (WR) Alabama State	1986
Gregory, Damian (DT) Illinois State	2002
Gregory, Jack (DE) Delta State	1967–71, 1979
Griffin, Don (CB) Middle Tennessee State	1994–95
Griffing, Glynn (QB) Mississippi	1964
Griffith, Robert (S) San Diego State	2002–04
Grigg, Forrest (DT) Tulsa	1948–51
Griggs, Anthony (LB) Ohio State	1986–88
Gross, Al (S) Arizona	1983–87
Groves, George (G) Marquette	1946
Groza, Lou (T, K) Ohio State	1946–59, 1961–67
Gruber, Bob (OT) Pittsburgh	1986
Guilbeau, Rusty (LB) McNeese State	1987

H

Hairston, Carl (DE) Maryland–East Shore	1984–89
Hairston, Stacey (DB) Ohio Northern	1993–94
Haley, Darryl (OL) Utah	*1987–88
Hall, Charlie (LB) Houston	1971–80
Hall, Dana (S) Washington	1995

Hall, Dino (KR, RB) Glassboro State	1979–83	Holcomb, Kelly (QB) Middle Tennessee State	2001–04
Haller, Alan (DB) Michigan State	1992	Holden, Steve (WR) Arizona State	1973–76
Ham, Derrick (DL) Miami (Florida)	2001	Holdman, Warrick (LB) Texas A&M	2004
Hambrick, Darren (LB) South Carolina	2002	Holland, Darius (DT) Colorado	1999–2000
Hamilton, Michael (LB) North Carolina A&T	2000	Holland, Jamie (WR) Ohio State	1992
Hannemann, Cliff (LB) Fresno State	*1987	Holloway, Glen (G) North Texas State	1974
Hansen, Brian (P) Sioux Falls	1991–93	Holmes, Earl (LB) Florida A&M	2002
Hanulak, Chet (RB) Maryland	1954, 1957	Holohan, Pete (TE) Notre Dame	1992
Harper, Mark (CB) Alcorn State	1986–90	Holt, Harry (TE) Arizona	1983–86
Harraway, Charley (RB) San Jose State	1966–68	Hooker, Fair (WR) Arizona State	1969–74
Harrington, John (DE) Marquette	1946	Hoover, Houston (G) Jackson State	1993
Harris, Antwan (DB) Virginia	###2005	Hopkins, Thomas (T) Alabama A&M	1983
Harris, Duriel (WR) New Mexico State	1984	Horn, Alvin (DB) Nevada–Las Vegas	*1987
Harris, Jon (DE) Virginia	#1999	Horn, Don (QB) San Diego State	1973
Harris, Josh (QB) Bowling Green	#2004	Horvath, Les (RB) Ohio State	1949
Harris, Marshall (DE) Texas Christian	1980–82	Houston, Jim (DE, LB) Ohio State	1960–72
Harris, Odie (DB) Sam Houston State	1991–92	Houston, Lin (G) Ohio State	1946–53
Hartley, Frank (TE) Illinois	1994–95	Howard, Sherman (RB) Nevada	1952–53
Harvey, Frank (FB) Georgia	##1994	Howell, Mike (DB) Grambling	1965–72
Haw, Brandon (DB) Rutgers	##2004	Howton, Bill (WR) Rice	1959
Hawkins, Ben (WR) Arizona State	1974	Humble, Weldon (LB) Rice	1947–50
Haynes, Hayward (OL) Florida State	##1991	Hunt, Bob (RB) Heidelberg	1974
Heiden, Steve (TE) South Dakota State	2002–05	Hunter, Art (C) Notre Dame	1956–59
Heinrich, Keith (TE) Sam Houston State	2003–04,	Hunter, Earnest (RB) Southeast	
	###2005	Oklahoma State	1995
Helluin, Jerry (DT) Tulane	1952–53	Hunter, Pete (DB) Virginia Union	2005
Henry, Anthony (DB) South Florida	2001–04	Hutchinson, Tom (WR) Kentucky	1963–65
Herring, Hal (LB) Auburn	1950–52	Hutchison, Chuck (G) Ohio State	1973–75
Herrion, Atlas (OL) Alabama	##2005	Huther, Bruce (LB) New Hampshire	1981
Hickerson, Gene (G) Mississippi	1958–60, 1962–73	Hybl, Nate (QB) Oklahoma	2003, ##2004
Hilgenberg, Jay (C) Iowa	1992	Hyder, Gaylon (OL) Texas Christian	2001
Hill, Calvin (RB) Yale	1978–81	Hynoski, Henry (RB) Temple	1975
Hill, Jim (DB) Texas A&I	1975		
Hill, Madre (RB) Arkansas	1999	**I**	
Hill, Travis (LB) Nebraska	1994–95	Ilgenfritz, Mark (DE) Vanderbilt	1974
Hill, Will (S) Bishop College	1988	Ingram, Darryl (TE) California	1991
Hilliard, Randy (CB) Louisiana State	1990–93	Irons, Gerald (LB) Maryland–East Shore	1976–79
Hoaglin, Fred (C) Pittsburgh	1966–72	Irons, Paul (TE) Florida State	2005
Hoard, Leroy (RB) Michigan	1990–95	Isaia, Sale (OL) UCLA	#1995
Hoffman, Andrew (DL) Virginia	##2005	Isbell, Joe Bob (G) Houston	1966
Hoggard, D. D. (CB) North Carolina State	1985–87	Israel, Ron (DB) Notre Dame	2003

J

Jackson, Alfred (DB) San Diego State	1991–92
Jackson, Bill (S) North Carolina	1982
Jackson, Corey (DL) Nevada	2003–04
Jackson, Enis (CB) Memphis State	*1987
Jackson, Frisman (WR) Western Illinois	2002–05
Jackson, James (RB) Miami (Florida)	2001–04
Jackson, Lenzie (WR) Arizona State	2000
Jackson, Michael (WR) Southern Mississippi	1991–95
Jackson, Raymond (DB) Colorado State	1999–2001
Jackson, Rich (DE) Southern	1972
Jackson, Robert E. (G) Duke	1975–85
Jackson, Robert L. (LB) Texas A&M	1978–81
Jacobs, Dave (K) Syracuse	1981
Jacobs, Tim (CB) Delaware	1993–95
Jaeger, Jeff (K) Washington	1987
Jagade, Harry (RB) Indiana	1951–53
James, Lynn (WR) Arizona State	1991
James, Nathaniel (DB) Florida A&M	1968
James, Tommy (DB) Ohio State	1948–55
Jameson, Michael (S) Texas A&M	2002–04
Jefferson, Ben (T) Maryland	##1989, 1990
Jefferson, John (WR) Arizona State	1985
Jenkins, Al (G) Tulsa	1969–70
Jennings, Brandon (DB) Texas A&M	#2001
Johnson, Bill (DL) Michigan State	1992–94
Johnson, Doug (QB) Florida	2005
Johnson, Eddie (LB) Louisville	1981–90
Johnson, Kevin (WR) Syracuse	1999–2003
Johnson, Lawrence (DB) Wisconsin	1979–84
Johnson, Lee (P) Brigham Young	1987–88
Johnson, Mark (LB) Missouri	1977
Johnson, Mike (LB) Virginia Tech	1986–93
Johnson, Mitch (T) UCLA	1971
Johnson, Pepper (LB) Ohio State	1993–95
Johnson, Ron (RB) Michigan	1969
Johnson, Tré (OL) Temple	2001
Johnson, Walter (DT) California State (Los Angeles)	1965–76
Joines, Vernon (WR) Maryland	1989–90
Jones, Bobby (WR) No College	1983

Jones, C. J. (WR) Iowa	#2003, ##2004
Jones, Dave (WR) Kansas State	1969–71
Jones, Dub (WR) Tulane	1948–55
Jones, Edgar (RB) Pittsburgh	1946–49
Jones, George (RB) San Diego State	1999
Jones, Homer (WR) Texas Southern	1970
Jones, James (DL) Northern Iowa	1991–94
Jones, Jock (LB) Virginia Tech	1990–91
Jones, Joe (DE) Tennessee State	1970–71, 1973, 1975–78
Jones, Keith (RB) Nebraska	1989
Jones, Kirk (RB) Nevada–Las Vegas	*1987
Jones, Lenoy (LB) Texas Christian	1999–2002
Jones, Marlon (DE) Central State	1987–89
Jones, Reginald (CB) Memphis State	#1994
Jones, Ricky (LB) Tuskegee	1977–79
Jones, Ricky (WR) Alabama State	##1992
Jones, Sean (DB) Georgia	2004–05
Jones, Selwyn (DB) Colorado State	1993, #1994
Jones, Tony (OT) Western Carolina	1988–95
Jordan, Henry (DT) Virginia	1957–58
Jordan, Homer (QB) Clemson	*1987
Junkin, Mike (LB) Duke	1987–88
Jurkovic, John (DT) Eastern Illinois	1999

K

Kafentzis, Mark (S) Hawaii	1982
Kanicki, Jim (DT) Michigan State	1963–69
Kapter, Alex (G) Northwestern	1946–47
Katolin, Mike (C) San Jose State	*1987
Kauric, Jerry (K) Kennedy Collegiate	1990
Kellermann, Ernie (DB) Miami (Ohio)	1966–71
Kelley, Chris (TE) Akron	*1987
Kelley, Ethan (DL) Baylor	2005
Kelly, Leroy (RB) Morgan State	1964–73
Kemp, Perry (WR) California (Pennsylvania)	*1987
Killian, P. J. (LB) Virginia	##1994
Killings, Cedric (DT) Carson-Newman	#2001
Kinard, Billy (DB) Mississippi	1956
Kinchen, Brian (TE) Louisiana State	1991–95
King, Andre (WR) Miami (Florida)	2001–04

King, Don (T) Kentucky	1954	Lewis, Cliff (QB) Duke	1946–51
King, Ed (OL) Auburn	1991–93	Lewis, Darryl (TE) Texas-Arlington	1984
King, Joe (DB) Oklahoma State	1991	Lewis, James (DB) Miami (Florida)	##2002
Kingrea, Rick (LB) Tulane	1971–72	Lewis, Leo (PR) Missouri	1990
Kirby, Terry (RB) Virginia	1999	Lewis, Stan (DE) Wayne State (Nebraska)	1975
Kirk, Randy (LB) San Diego State	1991	Lilja, George (G, T) Michigan	1984–86
Kissell, John (T) Boston College	1950–52, 1954–56	Linden, Errol (T) Houston	1961
Kmet, Frank (NT) Purdue	##1992	Lindsay, Everett (OL) Mississippi	2000
Kolesar, Bob (G) Michigan	1946	Lindsey, Dale (LB) Western Kentucky	1965–72
Konz, Ken (DB) Louisiana State	1953–59	Lindstrom, Gabe (P) Toledo	##2005
Kosar, Bernie (QB) Miami (Florida)	1985–93	Lingenfeiter, Bob (T) Nebraska	1977
Kosikowski, Frank (WR) Notre Dame	1948	Lingmerth, Goran (K) Northern Arizona	*1987
Kovaleski, Mike (LB) Notre Dame	*1987	Little, Earl (DB) Miami (Florida)	1999–2004
Kramer, Kyle (S) Bowling Green	1989	Littleton, Jody (S) Baylor	2005
Kreitling, Rich (WR) Illinois	1959–63	Lloyd, Dave (LB) Georgia	1959–61
Krerowicz, Mark (G) Ohio State	#1985	Lloyd, DeAngelo (DE) Tennessee	##2002
Kuechenberg, Rudy (LB) Indiana	1970	Logan, Dave (WR) Colorado	1976–83
Kuehl, Ryan (S) Virginia	1999–2002	Logan, Ernie (DL) East Carolina	1991–93
Kurpelkis, Justin (LB) Penn State	##2005	London, Tom (DB) North Carolina State	1978
Kyle, Jason (LB) Arizona State	1999	Long, Mel (LB) Toledo	1972–74
		Loomis, Ace (RB) LaCrosse State	1952
L		Lucci, Mike (LB) Tennessee	1962–64
Lacy, Bo (OL) Arkansas	#2004	Luck, Terry (QB) Nebraska	1977
Lahr, Warren (DB) Western Reserve	1948–59	Lund, Bill (RB) Case Tech	1946–47
LaMontagne, Noel (OL) Virginia	2000	Luneberg, Chris (OL) West Chester	##1993
Landry, George (RB) Lamar	*1987	Lyle, Rick (DE) Missouri	1994, #1995
Lane, Gary (QB) Missouri	1966–67	Lyons, Damion (DB) UCLA	##1994
Lang, Kenard (DL, LB) Miami (Florida)	2002–05	Lyons, Robert (S) Akron	1989
Langham, Antonio (CB) Alabama	1994–95, 1999		
Langhorne, Reggie (WR) Elizabeth City State	1985–91	**M**	
		Maceau, Mel (C) Marquette	1946–48
Lauter, Steve (S) San Diego State	*1987	Macerelli, John (G) St. Vincent	1956
Lavelli, Dante (WR) Ohio State	1946–56	Mack, Kevin (RB) Clemson	1985–93
Ledford, Dwayne (OL) East Carolina	2005	Maddox, Nick (RB) Florida State	2003
Lee, Barry (C) Grambling	*1987	Majors, Bobby (DB) Tennessee	1972
Lee, Marcus (RB) Syracuse	1994	Malbrough, Anthony (DB) Texas Tech	2000
Lefear, Billy (WR) Henderson State	1972–75	Malone, Ralph (DE) Georgia Tech	1986
Lehan, Michael (DB) Minnesota	2003–05	Manoa, Tim (FB) Penn State	1987–89
Leigh, Charles (RB) No College	1968–69	Marangi, Gary (QB) Boston College	#1977
Leomiti, Carlson (OL) San Diego State	##1994	Marshall, Dave (LB) Eastern Michigan	1984
LeVeck, Jack (LB) Ohio University	1975	Marshall, Jim (DE) Ohio State	1960

Martin, Jamie (QB) Weber State	#1999	Mercier, Richard (OL) Miami (Florida)	2001
Martin, Jim (DT) Notre Dame	1950	Metcalf, Eric (RB) Texas	1989–94
Mason, Larry (RB) Troy State	*1987	Meylan, Wayne (LB) Nebraska	1968–69
Massey, Carlton (DE) Texas	1954–56	Michaels, Walt (LB) Washington & Lee	1952–61
Matheson, Bob (LB) Duke	1967–70	Mickens, Ray (DB) Texas A&M	2005
Matthews, Clay (LB) Southern California	1978–93	Middleton, Ron (TE) Auburn	1989
Mayne, Lewis (RB) Texas	1947	Miller, Arnold (DL) Louisiana State	1999–2000
Mays, Dave (QB) Texas Southern	1976–77	Miller, Billy (TE) USC	2005
McCade, Mike (WR) Nevada–Las Vegas	*1987	Miller, Cleo (RB) Arkansas AM&N	1975–82
McCardell, Keenan (WR) Nevada–Las Vegas	1992–95	Miller, Jamir (LB) UCLA	1999–2001
McClung, Willie (DT) Florida A&M	1958–59	Miller, Mark (QB) Bowling Green	1978–79
McCollum, Andy (OL) Toledo	##1994	Miller, Matt (T) Colorado	1979–82
McCormack, Hurvin (DL) Indiana	1999	Miller, Nick (LB) Arkansas	1987
McCormack, Mike (T) Kansas	1954–62	Miller, Willie (WR) Colorado State	1975–76
McCown, Luke (QB) Louisiana Tech	2004	Milstead, Rod (G) Delaware State	#1993
McCullough, Sultan (RB) Southern California	##2004	Minniear, Randy (RB) Purdue	1970
McCusker, Jim (DE) Ohio State	1963	Minnifield, Frank (CB) Louisville	1984–92
McCutcheon, Daylon (CB) Southern California	1999–2005	Minter, Barry (LB) Tulsa	2001
		Mitchell, Alvin (DB) Morgan State	1968–69
McDonald, Paul (QB) Southern California	1980–85	Mitchell, Bobby (RB) Illinois	1958–61
McDonald, Tommy (WR) Oklahoma	1968	Mitchell, Mack (DE) Houston	1975–78
McGonnigal, Bruce (TE) Virginia	1991	Mitchell, Qasim (OL) North Carolina A&T	##2003
McIntyre, Corey (FB) West Virginia	##2004–05	Modzelewski, Dick (DT) Maryland	1964–66
McKay, Bob (T) Texas	1970–75	Modzelewski, Ed (RB) Maryland	1955–59
McKenzie, Keith (DE) Ball State	2000–01	Mohring, John (LB) C.W. Post	1980
McKenzie, Rich (DE) Penn State	1995	Monroe, Rod (TE) Cincinnati	##2000, 2001
McKinley, Alvin (DL) Mississippi State	2001–05	Montgomery, Cleotha (KR) Abilene Christian	1981
McKinney, Jeremy (T) Iowa	#1999, 2001	Moog, Aaron (DE) Nevada–Las Vegas	*1987
McKinnis, Hugh (RB) Arizona State	1973–75	Moore, Eric (OL) Indiana	1995
McLemore, Tom (TE) Southern	1993–94	Moore, Marty (LB) Kentucky	2000
McLeod, Kevin (FB) Auburn	2003	Moore, Stevon (DB) Mississippi	1992–95
McMahon, Jim (QB) Brigham Young	#1995	Moreland, Earthwind (DB) Georgia Southern	2001
McMahon, Pete (OL) Iowa	##2005		
McMillan, David (LB) Kansas	2005	Moreland, Jake (TE) Western Michigan	2001
McMillan, Erik (S) Missouri	1993	Moretti, David (LB) Oregon	##2003
McNeil, Clifton (WR) Grambling	1964–67	Morgan, Quincy (WR) Kansas State	2001–04
McNeil, Gerald (WR, KR) Baylor	1986–89	Moriarty, Pat (RB) Georgia Tech	1979
McNeil, Ryan (CB) Miami (Florida)	1999	Morin, Milt (TE) Massachusetts	1966–75
McTyer, Tim (S) Brigham Young	1999	Morris, Chris (T) Indiana	1972–73
Memmelaar, Dale (G) Wyoming	1964–65	Morris, Joe (RB) Syracuse	1991

Morris, Mike (C) Northeast Mississippi State	1990	Nugent, Terry (QB) Colorado State	#1984
Morrison, Fred (RB) Ohio State	1954–56	Nutting, Ed (DT) Georgia Tech	1961
Morrison, Reece (RB) Southwest Texas State	1968–72	**O**	
Morrow, Alvin (TE) None	#2001, ##2002	Oakley, Anthony (OL) Western Kentucky	##2004
Morrow, John (C) Michigan	1960–66	Oben, Roman (OT) Louisville	2000–01
Morton, Christian (DB) Illinois	##2004	O'Brien, Francis (T) Michigan State	1959
Morze, Frank (C) Boston College	1962–63	O'Connell, Tom (QB) Illinois	1956–57
Moseley, Mark (K) Stephen F. Austin	1986	O'Connor, Bill (DE) Notre Dame	1949
Moselle, Dom (RB) Superior State College (Wisconsin)	1950	O'Connor, Drew (WR) Maine	##2000
Mosley, Kendrick (WR) Western Michigan	##2005	Oden, McDonald (TE) Tennessee State	1980–82
Mostardi, Richard (DB) Kent State	1960	Odom, Clifton (LB) Texas-Arlington	1980
Motley, Marion (RB) Nevada	1946–53	Ogle, Kendall (LB) Maryland	1999
Murphy, Fred (WR) Georgia Tech	1960	O'Hara, Shaun (OL) Rutgers	2000–03
Mustafa, Isaiah (WR) Arizona State	##1999	Oliphant, Mike (RB) Puget Sound	1989–91
Mustafaa, Najee (CB) Georgia Tech	1993	Oliver, Bob (DE) Abilene Christian	1969
Mustard, Chad (TE) North Dakota	##2002, 2003–04	Oristaglio, Bob (DE) Pennsylvania	1951
		Osborne, Scot (OL) William & Mary	#2003
Myers, Michael (DL) Alabama	2003–04	Osika, Craig (OL) Indiana	2003–04
Myles, Toby (OL) Jackson State	2001	Owens, Kerry (LB) Arkansas	##1989
Myslinski, Tom (OL) Tennessee	##1992	**P**	
		Pagel, Mike (QB) Arizona State	1986–90
N		Palelei, Lonnie (OL) Nevada-Las Vegas	#1995
		Palmer, Derrell (DT) Texas Christian	1949–53
Nagler, Gern (WR) Santa Clara	1960–61	Palmer, Randy (TE) Texas A&M-Kingsville	1999
Nave, Stevan (LB) Kansas	*1987	Palumbo, Sam (LB) Notre Dame	1955–56
Nelsen, Bill (QB) Southern California	1968–72	Parilli, Vito (QB) Kentucky	1956
Neujahr, Quentin (OL) Kansas State	#1995	Parker, Frank (DT) Oklahoma State	1962–64, 1966–67
Newman, Patrick (WR) San Diego State	1994	Parker, Jerry (LB) Central State	*1987
Newsome, Ozzie (TE) Alabama	1978–90	Parker, J'Vonne (DL) Rutgers	2005
Newsome, Vince (DB) Washington	1991–92	Parris, Gary (TE) Florida State	1975–78
Nicolas, Scott (LB) Miami	1982–86	Parrish, Bernie (DB) Florida	1959–66
Nimmo, Lance (OL) West Virginia	##2004	Parseghian, Ara (RB) Miami (Ohio)	1948–49
Ninowski, Jim (QB) Michigan State	1958–59, 1962–66	Patten, David (WR) Western Carolina	2000
		Patten, Joel (T) Duke	1980
Nix, John (DL) Southern Mississippi	#2003	Paul, Don (DB) Washington State	1954–58
Noa, Kaulana (OL) Hawaii	##2002	Payton, Eddie (KR) Jackson State	1977
Noll, Chuck (G, LB) Dayton	1953–59	Pearson, Kalvin (DB) Grambling	2002
Northcutt, Dennis (WR) Arizona	2000–05	Pederson, Doug (QB) Northeast Louisiana	2000

Peebles, Danny (WR) North Carolina State	1991	Ptacek, Bob (QB) Michigan	1959
Pena, Bob (G) Massachusetts	1972	Pucci, Ben (DT) No College	1948
Perini, Pete (RB) Ohio State	1955	Pucillo, Mike (OL) Auburn	2005
Perkins, Antonio (DB) Oklahoma	2005	Pupua, Tau (DT) Weber State	#1995
Perry, Michael Dean (DT) Clemson	1988–94	Putnam, Duane (G) College of Pacific	1961
Perry, Rod (CB) Colorado	1983–84	Puzzuoli, Dave (NT) Pittsburgh	1983–87
Peters, Floyd (DT) San Francisco State	1959–62	Pyne, Jim (G) Virginia Tech	1999–2000
Peters, Tony (DB) Oklahoma	1975–78		
Petersen, Ted (T) Eastern Illinois	1984	**Q**	
Petitbon, John (DB) Notre Dame	1955–56	Quinlan, Bill (DE) Michigan State	1957–58
Petruziello, Dave (OL) Michigan	##2003	Quinlan, Voiney (RB) San Diego State	1956
Phelps, Don (RB) Kentucky	1950–51	Quinton, Dustin (OL) Nevada–Las Vegas	##1991
Phenix, Perry (DB) Southern Mississippi	#2001		
Philcox, Todd (QB) Syracuse	1991–93	**R**	
Phipps, Mike (QB) Purdue	1970–76	Raimey, Dave (DB) Michigan	1964
Pierce, Calvin (FB) Eastern Illinois	*1987	Rainer, Wali (LB) Virginia	1999–2001
Pierce, Steve (WR) Illinois	*1987	Rakoczy, Gregg (OL) Miami	1987–90
Pietrosante, Nick (RB) Notre Dame	1966–67	Ratterman, George (QB) Notre Dame	1952–56
Pike, Chris (DL) Tulsa	1989–90	Rechichar, Bert (DB) Tennessee	1952
Piskor, Ray (T) Niagara	1947	Redden, Barry (RB) Richmond	1989–90
Pittman, Thomas (DL) Florida	##2003	Reeves, Ken (OL) Texas A&M	1990
Pitts, Frank (WR) Southern	1971–73	Reeves, Walter (TE) Auburn	1994–95
Pitts, John (DB) Arizona State	1975	Rehberg, Scott (OL) Central Michigan	1999
Pizzo, Joe (QB) Mars Hill	*1987	Renfro, Ray (WR) North Texas State	1952–63
Pleasant, Anthony (DE) Tennessee State	1990–95	Reynolds, Billy (RB) Pittsburgh	1953–54, 1957
Plum, Milt (QB) Penn State	1957–61	Reynolds, Chuck (C) Tulsa	1969–70
Polley, Tom (LB) Nevada–Las Vegas	*1987	Rhett, Errict (RB) Florida	2000
Pontbriand, Ryan (S) Rice	2003–05	Rhome, Jerry (QB) Tulsa	1969
Pool, Brodney (DB) Oklahoma	2005	Rich, Randy (DB) New Mexico	1978–79
Poole, Larry (RB) Kent State	1975–77	Richardson, Gloster (WR) Jackson State	1972–74
Pope, Marquez (S) Fresno State	1999	Richardson, Kyle (P) Arkansas State	2005
Poumele, Pulu (G) Arizona	##1995	Rideau, Brandon (WR) Kansas	##2005
Powell, Craig (LB) Ohio State	1995	Riddick, Louis (DB) Pittsburgh	1993–95
Powell, Preston (RB) Grambling	1961	Rienstra, John (OL) Temple	1991–92
Powell, Ronnie (WR) Northwestern State	1999	Righetti, Joe (DT) Waynesburg	1969–70
Powers, Ricky (RB) Michigan	1995	Risien, Cody (T) Texas A&M	1979–83,
Prentice, Travis (RB) Miami (Ohio)	2000		1985–89
Prestel, Jim (T) Idaho	1960	Rison, Andre (WR) Michigan State	1995
Pritchett, Billy (RB) West Texas State	1975	Roan, Oscar (TE) Southern Methodist	1975–78
Pruitt, Greg (RB) Oklahoma	1973–81	Robbins, Kevin (OT) Michigan State	##1989, 1990
Pruitt, Mike (RB) Purdue	1976–84	Roberts, Walter (WR) San Jose State	1964–66

Robinson, Billy (DB) Arizona State	*1987	Schoen, Tom (DB) Notre Dame	1970
Robinson, DeJuan (DB) Northern Arizona	*1987	Schultz, Randy (RB) State College (Iowa)	1966
Robinson, Fred (G) Washington	1957	Schwenk, Bud (QB) Washington	1946
Robinson, Mike (DE) Arizona	1981–82	Scott, Bo (RB) Ohio State	1969–74
Rockins, Chris (S) Oklahoma State	1984–87	Scott, Cedric (DE) Southern Mississippi	2002
Rogers, Don (S) UCLA	1984–85	Scott, Clarence (DB) Kansas State	1971–83
Rogers, Tyrone (DL) Alabama State	1999–2004	Sczurek, Stan (LB) Purdue	1963–65
Rokisky, John (DE) Duquesne	1946	Seifert, Mike (DE) Wisconsin	1974
Roman, Nick (DE) Ohio State	1972–74	Selawski, Gene (T) Purdue	1960
Romaniszyn, Jim (LB) Edinboro State	1973–74	Sellers, Mike (HB) Walla Walla	
Roso, Ken (LB) Nevada–Las Vegas	1990	Community College	2001
Rouson, Lee (RB) Colorado	1991	Sensanbaugher, Dean (RB) Ohio State	1948
Rowe, Patrick (WR) San Diego State	1993	Sharkey, Ed (G) Nevada	1952
Rowell, Eugene (WR) Southern Mississippi	1990	Sharpe, Ricky (DB) San Diego State	##2004
Roye, Orpheus (DL) Florida State	2000–05	Shavers, Tyrone (WR) Lamar	1991
Rucker, Reggie (WR) Boston University	1975–81	Shaw, Sedrick (RB) Iowa	1999
Rudd, Dwayne (LB) Alabama	2001–02	Shea, Aaron (TE) Michigan	2000–05
Ruff, Orlando (LB) Furman	2005	Shelton, L. J. (OL) Eastern Michigan	2005
Ruhman, Chris (OL) Texas A&M	1999	Shepard, Gannon (OL) Duke	##2001
Runager, Max (P) South Carolina	1988	Shepherd, Leslie (WR) Temple	1999
Rusinek, Mike (NT) California	*1987	Sheppard, Henry (G, T) Southern	
Russell, Brian (DB) San Diego State	2005	Methodist	1976–81
Ryan, Frank (QB) Rice	1962–68	Sheriff, Stan (G) California Poly	1957
Rymkus, Lou (T) Notre Dame	1946–51	Sherk, Jerry (DT) Oklahoma State	1970–81
Rypien, Mark (QB) Washington State	1994	Shiner, Dick (QB) Maryland	1967
		Shoals, Roger (T) Maryland	1963–64
S		Shofner, Jim (DB) Texas Christian	1958–63
Saban, Lou (LB) Indiana	1946–49	Shorter, Jim (DB) Detroit	1962–63
Sabatino, Bill (DT) Colorado	1968	Shula, Don (DB) John Carroll	1951–52
Sagapolutele, Pio (DL) Hawaii	1991–95	Shurnas, Marshall (WR) Missouri	1947
St. Clair, Mike (DE) Grambling	1976–79	Sikich, Mike (G) Northwestern	1971
Salaam, Rashaan (RB) Colorado	1999	Sikora, Robert (T) Indiana	#1984
Saleh, Tarek (LB, FB) Wisconsin	1999–2001	Simmons, Tony (WR) Wisconsin	2001
Sanders, Darnell (TE) Ohio State	2002–03	Simonetti, Len (DT) Tennessee	1946–48
Sanders, Lewis (DB) Maryland	2000–04	Simons, Kevin (OT) Tennessee	##1989
Sandusky, John (T) Villanova	1950–55	Sims, Darryl (DE) Wisconsin	*1987–88
Sanford, Lucius (LB) Georgia Tech	1987	Sims, Mickey (DT) South Carolina State	1977–79
Santiago, O. J. (TE) Kent State	#2000, 2001	Sipe, Brian (QB) San Diego State	1974–83
Scales, Charley (RB) Indiana	1962–65	Skibinski, Joe (G) Purdue	1952
Scarry, Mike (C) Waynesburg	1946–47	Skinner, Webster (WR) San Diego State	1986–91
Schafrath, Dick (G, T) Ohio State	1959–71	Slayden, Steve (QB) Duke	#1988

Smith, Bob (LB) Nebraska	1955–56
Smith, Clifton (LB) Syracuse	##2005
Smith, Daryle (OT) Tennessee	1989
Smith, Gaylon (RB) Southwestern	1946
Smith, Irv (TE) Notre Dame	1999
Smith, Jim Ray (G) Baylor	1956–62
Smith, John (WR) Tennessee State	1979
Smith, Ken (TE) New Mexico	1973
Smith, Leroy (LB) Iowa	##1992
Smith, Mark (DL) Auburn	2001–02
Smith, Marquis (S) California	1999–2001
Smith, Ralph (TE) Mississippi	1965–68
Smith, Rico (WR) Colorado	1992–95
Smith, Terrelle (FB) Arizona State	2004–05
Snellings, Paul (OL) Georgia	#2000
Snidow, Ron (DE) Oregon	1968–72
Sommersell, Andre (LB) Colorado State	##2004
Sparenberg, Dave (G) Western Ontario	*1987
Speedie, Mac (WR) Utah	1946–52
Speegle, Nick (LB) New Mexico	2005
Speer, Del (S) Florida	1993–94
Spencer, Joe (DT) Oklahoma State	1949
Spikes, Rahshon (RB) North Carolina State	##2000
Spires, Greg (DL) Florida State	2001
Spragan, Donnie (LB) Stanford	##2001
Spriggs, Marcus (DL) Troy State	1999–2000, #2001
Stafford, Shane (QB) Connecticut	##2002
Stams, Frank (LB) Notre Dame	1992–95
Stanfield, Harold (TE) West Virginia Tech	*1987
Staroba, Paul (WR) Michigan	1972
Steinbrunner, Don (DE) Washington State	1953
Stephens, Larry (DT) Texas	1960–61
Steuber, Bob (RB) Missouri	1946
Stevenson, Rickey (CB) Arizona	1970
Stewart, Andrew (DE) Cincinnati	1989
Stewart, Matt (LB) Vanderbilt	2005
Stienke, Jim (DB) Southwest Texas State	1973
Stokes, Barry (OL) Eastern Michigan	2002–03
Stoutmire, Omar (DB) Fresno State	#1999
Stover, Matt (K) Louisiana State	1991–95
Stracka, Tim (TE) Wisconsin	1983–84

Strock, Don (QB) Virginia Tech	1988
Suggs, Lee (RB) Virginia Tech	2003–05
Sullivan, Dave (WR) Virginia	1973–74
Sullivan, Gerry (T, C) Illinois	1974–81
Sullivan, Tom (RB) Miami (Florida)	1978
Summers, Fred (DB) Wake Forest	1969–71
Sumner, Walt (DB) Florida State	1969–74
Sumter, Glenn (DB) Memphis	##2002
Sustersic, Ed (RB) Findlay	1949
Sutter, Ed (LB) Northwestern	##1992, 1993–95
Swarn, George (RB) Miami (Ohio)	*1987
Swilling, Ken (LB) Georgia Tech	##1992
Sykes, Terrance (OL) Louisiana Tech	#2001

T

Taffoni, Joe (T) Tennessee-Martin	1967–70
Talley, John (TE) West Virginia	##1989, 1990–91
Tamm, Ralph (G) West Chester State	1990–91
Taseff, Carl (DB) John Carroll	1951
Taylor, Ben (LB) Virginia Tech	2002–05
Taylor, Ryan (LB) Auburn	##1999–2000
Taylor, Terry (CB) Southern Illinois	1992–93
Teets, Dick (LB) Wisconsin	*1987
Teifke, Mike (C) Akron	*1987
Tennell, Derek (TE) UCLA	*1987–89
Terlep, George (QB) Notre Dame	1948
Terrell, Ray (RB) Mississippi	1946–47
Testaverde, Vinny (QB) Miami (Florida)	1993–95
Thaxton, Jim (TE) Tennessee State	1974
Thierry, John (LB, DE) Alcorn State	1999
Thomas, Johnny (CB) Baylor	1995
Thome, Chris (OL) Minnesota	1991–92
Thompson, Bennie (DB) Grambling	1994–95
Thompson, Chaun (LB) West Texas A&M	2003–05
Thompson, David (DL) Ohio State	##2003
Thompson, Kevin (QB) Penn State	2000, #2002
Thompson, Mike (DT) Wisconsin	1999–2000
Thompson, Tommy (LB) William & Mary	1949–53
Thornton, James (DB) Morris Brown	##2005
Thornton, John (DL) Cincinnati	1991
Tidmore, Sam (LB) Ohio State	1962–63

Tierney, Leo (C) Georgia Tech	1978
Tillman, Lawyer (WR) Auburn	1989, 1992–93
Tinsley, Keith (WR) Pittsburgh	*1987
Toles, Deryck (TE) Penn State	##2004
Tomczak, Mike (QB) Ohio State	1992
Trocano, Rick (DB, QB) Pittsburgh	1981–83
Trumbull, Rick (OL) Missouri	##1991
Tucker, Ryan (OT) Texas Christian	2002–05
Tucker, Travis (TE) Southern Connecticut State	1985–87
Tupa, Tom (QB, P) Ohio State	#1993, 1994–95
Turnbow, Jesse (DT) Tennessee	1978
Turner, Eric (S) UCLA	1991–95
Turner, Kevin (LB) Pacific	1982

U

Ulinski, Ed (G) Marshall	1946–49
Unck, Mason (LB) Arizona State	2003–05
Upshaw, Marvin (DE) Trinity	1968–69

V

Van Dyke, Ralph (T) Southern Illinois	*1987
Van Pelt, Brad (LB) Michigan State	1986
Vardell, Tommy (RB) Stanford	1992–95
Verba, Ross (OL) Iowa	2001–02, 2004
Verser, David (WR) Kansas	*1987

W

Wagner, Bryan (P) Cal State–Northridge	1989–90
Waiters, Van (LB) Indiana	1988–91
Walker, Dwight (RB, WR) Nicholls State	1982–84
Wallace, Calvin (DE) West Virginia Tech	*1987
Walls, Everson (DB) Grambling	1992–93
Walls, Raymond (DB) Southern Mississippi	2002
Walters, Dale (P) Rice	*1987
Ward, Carl (DB) Michigan	1967–68
Ward, Chad (OL) Washington	##2002
Warfield, Paul (WR) Ohio State	1964–69, 1976–77
Warren, Gerard (DL) Florida	2001–04
Washington, Brian (S) Nebraska	1988
Washington, Marcus (DB) Colorado	##1999

Watkins, Tom (RB) Iowa State	1961
Watson, Karlton (QB) Winston-Salem	*1987
Watson, Louis (WR) Mississippi Valley State.	*1987
Watson, Remi (WR) Bethune-Cookman	*1987
Weathers, Clarence (WR) Delaware State	1985–88
Weathers, Curtis (TE, LB) Mississippi	1979–85
Webb, Ken (RB) Presbyterian	1963
Weber, Chuck (DE) West Chester State	1955–56
Webster, Larry (DT) Maryland	1995
Westmoreland, Eric (LB) Tennessee	2004
White, Bob (RB) Stanford	1955
White, Charles (RB) Southern California	1980–82, 1984
White, Jamal (LB) Kentucky	##2002
White, Jamel (RB) South Dakota	2000–03
White, James (DE) Louisiana State	#1985
White, Lorenzo (RB) Michigan State	1995
Whitlow, Bob (C) Arizona	1968
Whitwell, Mike (WR, S) Texas A&M	1982–83
Wiggin, Paul (DE) Stanford	1957–67
Wilburn, Barry (CB) Mississippi	1992
Wilkerson, Gary (DB) Penn State	##1989
Wilkinson, Jerry (DE) Oregon State	1980
Williams, A. D. (WR) College of Pacific	1960
Williams, Arthur (WR) Abilene Christian	*1987
Williams, Clarence (RB) Washington State	1993
Williams, Gene (T, G) Iowa State	1993–94
Williams, James (LB) Mississippi State	1999
Williams, Larry (G) Notre Dame	1986–88
Williams, Lawrence (KR) Texas Tech	1977
Williams, Ray (WR) Clemson	*1987
Williams, Roosevelt (DB) Tuskegee	2003
Williams, Sidney (LB) Southern	1964–66
Williams, Stacy (DB) East Texas State	*1987
Williams, Tony (T) Kansas State	1993
Williams, Wally (C) Florida A&M	1993–95
Willis, Bill (G, LB) Ohio State	1946–53
Willis, Keith (TE) Virginia Tech	##2004
Wilson, Tom (RB) No College	1962
Wilson, Troy (CB) Notre Dame	*1987
Wingle, Blake (G) UCLA	*1987

Winslow, George (P) Villanova — 1987

Winslow, Kellen (TE) Miami (Florida) — 2004–@05

Winters, Frank (C) Western Illinois — 1987–88

Wise, Mike (DL) California–Davis — 1991

Wiska, Jeff (G) Michigan State — 1986

Wohlabaugh, Dave (C) Syracuse — 1999–2002

Wolfley, Ron (RB) West Virginia — 1992–93

Woods, Rob (OL) Arizona — 1991

Woolsey, Rolly (DB) Boise State — 1977

Wooten, John (G) Colorado — 1959–67

Word, Mark (DE) Jacksonville State — 2002–03

Wren, Junior (DB) Missouri — 1956–59

Wright, Alvin (NT) Jacksonville State — 1992

Wright, Felix (S) Drake — 1985–90

Wright, George (DT) Sam Houston — 1972

Wright, Jason (RB) Northwestern — 2005

Wright, Keith (WR, KR) Memphis State — 1978–80

Wycinsky, Craig (G) Michigan State — 1972

Wynn, Spergon (QB) Southwest Texas State — 2000

Y

Yanchar, Bill (DT) Purdue — 1970

Yonakor, John (DE) Notre Dame — 1946–49

Young, David (DB) Georgia
Southern — ##2003

Young, George (DE) Georgia — 1946–53

Young, Glen (WR) Mississippi — 1984–85, 1987–88

Youngblood, George (DB) California
State–Los Angeles — 1967

Youngelman, Sid (DT) Alabama — 1959

Yovanovits, Dave (OL) Temple — 2005

Z

Zahursky, Steve (OL) Kent State — 1999–2000

Zeier, Eric (QB) Georgia — 1995

Zeno, Lance (C) UCLA — 1992–93

Ziegler, Doug (TE) Mississippi — ##2004

Zukauskas, Paul (OL) Boston College — 2001–04

Notes

Paul Brown: A Remarkable Life in Football

"Most Memorable Games (According to Paul Brown in his autobiography..." Brown, Paul, *PB: The Paul Brown Story*, New York: Antheneum, 1979.

"Everything had to do with people—from properly assessing a man's character..." Brown, Paul, *PB: The Paul Brown Story*, New York: Antheneum, 1979.

Otto Graham—The Browns' First Superstar

"The first time I ever saw Otto Graham play football, for instance, was in our 14–7 loss to Pappy Waldorf's Northwestern team..." Brown, Paul, *PB: The Paul Brown Story*, New York: Antheneum, 1979.

Equal Opportunity

"I never considered football players black or white." Brown, Paul, *PB: The Paul Brown Story*, New York: Antheneum, 1979.

"Ralph [Webster] was very impressed with the manner in which we treated our black players at Massillon..." Brown, Paul, *PB: The Paul Brown Story*, New York: Antheneum, 1979.

"Both men handled this sensitive situation with great dignity and understanding..." Brown, Paul, *PB: The Paul Brown Story*, New York: Antheneum, 1979.

Making an Impression in the NFL: The 1950 Championship Season

"That was the game I remember most..." Bob Dolgan, "Otto Graham 1921–2003 Former Browns QB Led Team to Dominance with Seven League Titles," *The* (Cleveland) *Plain Dealer*, December 18, 2003.

"We trapped them to death..." Harry Jones, "Trap Snaps on Steller Line," *The* (Cleveland) *Plain Dealer*, October 30, 1950.

"I've been scared to death for a week..." Harry Jones, "Browns Pressed, but Take Starch Out of Marshall, Ex-Laundryman," *The* (Cleveland) *Plain Dealer*, November 20, 1950.

"Don't worry, Otts. We're still..." Bob Dolgan, "There was never a game like this," *The* (Cleveland) *Plain Dealer*, December 24, 2000.

"This is the gamest bunch of guys in the world..." Bob Dolgan, "There was never a game like this," *The* (Cleveland) *Plain Dealer*, December 24, 2000.

The Man with the Hands: Dante Lavelli

"More than 50 years ago, we original Browns established something unique..." Dante Lavelli, foreword to *The Cleveland Browns: The Great Tradition,* 3rd rev. ed., by Bob Moon (Columbus, OH: SporTradition Publications, 1999).

"I can't remember his dropping a single pass during the 11 seasons he played with the Browns..." Brown, Paul, *PB: The Paul Brown Story,* New York: Antheneum, 1979.

The 1954 Championship Season

"We looked considerably better..." Chuck Heaton, "Bassett Smashes for Two Scores," *The* (Cleveland) *Plain Dealer,* October 25, 1954.

"That Ratterman is a good one..." Chuck Heaton, "Connects 10 of 11 Passes for Three TDs," *The* (Cleveland) *Plain Dealer,* November 8, 1954.

"The finest football team I've ever coached on a given day..." Chuck Heaton, "Browns Regain Title, 56–10," *The* (Cleveland) *Plain Dealer,* December 27, 1954.

"I saw it, but still hardly can believe it..." Chuck Heaton, "Browns Regain Title, 56–10," *The* (Cleveland) *Plain Dealer,* December 27, 1954.

Lou Groza: Always There in the Clutch

"I know that Lou won more games in clutch situations..." Brown, Paul, *PB: The Paul Brown Story,* New York: Antheneum, 1979.

"Where would I have been if he hadn't have seen me playing basketball..." Natali, Alan, *Brown's Town: 20 Famous Browns Talk amongst Themselves,* Wilmington, OH: Orange Frazer Press, 2001.

The 1955 Championship Season

"The little man beat us personally..." Chuck Heaton, "LeBaron's Three Touchdowns Shatter Jinx," *The* (Cleveland) *Plain Dealer,* September 26, 1955.

"There is no doubt that Graham's late arrival made it difficult..." "Ratterman Hikes Rating as Passer," *The* (Cleveland) *Plain Dealer,* September 26, 1955.

"How well we recover from our injuries will decide whether we can stay in contention..." "Recovery from Injuries Is Key to Browns' Fate," *The* (Cleveland) *Plain Dealer,* November 14, 1955.

Jim Brown: A Hero on the Field, a Star on the Big Screen

"The keys to his success were that rare combination of strength and speed..." Brown, Paul, *PB: The Paul Brown Story,* New York: Antheneum, 1979.

The Controversial Art Modell

"The darkest period of my life." Brown, Paul, *PB: The Paul Brown Story,* New York: Antheneum, 1979.

The 1964 Championship Season

"I don't feel I did very well..." Chuck Such, "Browns Victory over Dallas Costly," *The* (Canton) *Repository,* October 5, 1964.

"Our winning combination today was excellent balance..." Chuck Such, "Cleveland Eyes Upcoming 'Toughies' after 34–24 Win," *The* (Canton) *Repository,* November 9, 1964.

"This was the type of aggressive football we've been wanting..." Bill School, "Keep December 27 Open, Browns Fans," *Cleveland Press,* November 16, 1964.

"They gambled on that pass, and it paid off for them..." Charles Heaton, "Parrish Shoulders Blame for Gamble," *The* (Cleveland) *Plain Dealer,* November 23, 1964.

"Cleveland looks like a championship team to me..." Bill Scholl, "Packer Pilot Says Browns Look Like Title-Bound Club," *Cleveland Press,* November 23, 1964.

"The Cardinals took advantage of their opportunities..." Charles Heaton, "We Couldn't Make Big Plays —Collier," *The* (Cleveland) *Plain Dealer,* December 7, 1964.

"We're going to win the title in my old hometown..." Chuck Such, "Browns Suffer from St. Louis Blues, Lose, 20–19," *The* (Canton) *Repository,* December 7, 1964.

"That has to be the greatest game Frank Ryan..." Russell Schneider, "Ryan Was at His Best Is Unanimous Viewpoint," *The* (Cleveland) *Plain Dealer,* December 13, 1964.

"Any quarterback can call a helluva game..." Russell Schneider, "Ryan Was at His Best Is Unanimous Viewpoint," *The* (Cleveland) *Plain Dealer,* December 13, 1964.

"It was the best defensive game of the year..." Associated Press, "Cleveland Blitz Leave Colts in Ruins," *The New York Times,* December 20, 1964.

"It's the biggest thrill of my career..." Charles Heaton, "'My Biggest Thrill' Says Brown," *The* (Cleveland) *Plain Dealer,* December 20, 1964.

"We live in a country where a man can worship..." Jim Brown, "Cassius and the Black Muslims Not Grave Threat to Country," *The* (Cleveland) *Plain Dealer,* May 31, 1964.

"I'm not trying to change his mind, but I class it as a sport..." Jim Brown, "He Disagrees with Our Leader on the Subject of Golf Being a Sport," *The* (Cleveland) *Plain Dealer,* June 7, 1964.

Monday Night Football

"I'm a Joe Namath fan..." Dan Coughlin, "Browns Hail Namath," *The* (Cleveland) *Plain Dealer,* September 22, 1970.

"Namath is one of the great all-time passers..." Dan Coughlin, "Browns Hail Namath," *The* (Cleveland) *Plain Dealer,* September 22, 1970.

"There is nothing I can say after a losing game..." Tom Place, "Browns Strong—Joe," *The* (Cleveland) *Plain Dealer,* September 22, 1970.

A Rust Belt Rivalry—The Steelers versus the Browns

"Nock nock. Whu's dere?" Start Page, *The* (Cleveland) *Plain Dealer,* October 5, 2003.

"Steelers fans=senses falter." John Campanelli, "Sports Rival Anagrams," *The* (Cleveland) *Plain Dealer,* November 14, 2004.

A Boy from Brooklyn Makes Good: Sam Rutigliano

"I grew up in New York City..." clevelandseniors.com

A Champion at Any Age: Brian Sipe

"I had so much fun working with the kids and smelling the grass again..." Steve Brand and Bill Dickens, "Sipe Named Head Coach at Santa Fe Christian; Former Star Says Love of Football Rekindled," *The San Diego Union-Tribune,* January 19, 2001.

"I don't want to sound heroic..." Marla Ridenour, "Excitement Back for Sipe, Ex-Brown Returns as Prep Coach," *Akron Beacon Journal,* November 7, 2001.

"I think I'm one of the very few who played on a [Little League] championship..." Nick Canepa, "Brian Sipe Will Never Pass on Williamsport Memories," *The San Diego Union-Tribune,* August 18, 2005.

Kardiac Arrest

"I'm going to give Sam Rutigliano the benefit of the doubt..." Hal Lebovitz, "Pass? Browns Had to Try Field Goal," *The* (Cleveland) *Plain Dealer,* January 5, 1981.

"We felt a field goal was no gut cinch..." Russ Schneider, "Kardiac Kids Run Out of Miracles," *The* (Cleveland) *Plain Dealer,* January 5, 1981.

"I thought we would run the ball and in so doing set up a field goal..." Russ Schneider, "Kardiac Kids Run Out of Miracles," *The* (Cleveland) *Plain Dealer,* January 5, 1981.

"I was behind Davis and then Burgess Owens came back to me..." Russ Schneider, "Kardiac Kids Run Out of Miracles," *The* (Cleveland) *Plain Dealer,* January 5, 1981.

"It was not the play; it was the execution that was bad..." Russ Schneider, "Kardiac Kids Run Out of Miracles," *The* (Cleveland) *Plain Dealer,* January 5, 1981.

"I was surprised he threw in that situation..." *The* (Cleveland) *Plain Dealer,* January 5, 1981.

"I was open..." *The* (Cleveland) *Plain Dealer,* January 5, 1981.

"Yes, I have feelings of regret..." Russ Schneider, "Sipe Regrets Sad Ending to Good Year," *The* (Cleveland) *Plain Dealer,* January 5, 1981.

"There is no toughest thing..." Russ Schneider, "Kardiac Kids Run Out of Miracles," *The* (Cleveland) *Plain Dealer,* January 5, 1981.

The Drive

"Whenever you have John Elway as your quarterback..." Bill Livingston, "37 Seconds Too Long, Great Season for Browns Ends Bitterly in Overtime," *The* (Cleveland) *Plain Dealer,* January 12, 1987.

"I tried to get to Pasadena during my whole college career..." Gene Williams, "Broncos Buck Long Odds as Elway Silences Critics," *The* (Cleveland) *Plain Dealer,* January 12, 1987.

"I told them we had plenty of time..." George Sweda, "Different Refrain This Time," *The* (Cleveland) *Plain Dealer,* January 12, 1987.

"We play best when our backs are to the wall. ..." Gene Williams, "Broncos Buck Long Odds as Elway Silences Critics," *The* (Cleveland) *Plain Dealer,* January 12, 1987.

"If you work hard, good things are going to happen..." Gene Williams, "Broncos Buck Long Odds as Elway Silences Critics," *The* (Cleveland) *Plain Dealer,* January 12, 1987.

"That gave us some breathing room..." George Sweda, "Different Refrain This Time," *The* (Cleveland) *Plain Dealer,* January 12, 1987.

"There were two options on the play..." George Sweda, "Different Refrain This Time," *The* (Cleveland) *Plain Dealer,* January 12, 1987.

"There were others, but that may have been the most important..." Chuck Heaton, "Browns Didn't Change Defense, Coach Says," *The* (Cleveland) *Plain Dealer,* January 12, 1987.

"I saw no pressure on John at all..." Elton Alexander, "In the End, Broncos Just Romped in the Wide-Open Spaces," *The* (Cleveland) *Plain Dealer,* January 12, 1987.

"I was trying to get outside, to turn it up..." Tony Grossi, "Broncos End Browns' Dream, 23–20," *The* (Cleveland) *Plain Dealer,* January 12, 1987.

"If I had taken another step backward, I think I would have had it..." Bob Dolgan, "Overtime Loss a Bitter Pill to Swallow for Browns," *The* (Cleveland) *Plain Dealer,* January 12, 1987.

"I got around Hanford [Dixon] with a pretty clean release..." Elton Alexander, "In the End, Broncos Just Romped in the Wide-Open Spaces," *The* (Cleveland) *Plain Dealer,* January 12, 1987.

"We were in zone coverage..." Bob Dolgan, "Overtime Loss a Bitter Pill to Swallow for Browns," *The* (Cleveland) *Plain Dealer,* January 12, 1987.

"I made it by about a foot inside that left post..." Elton Alexander, "Karlis Looked Up in Hurry," *The* (Cleveland) *Plain Dealer,* January 12, 1987.

"The way we did it, it was so awesome..." George Sweda, "Different Refrain This Time," *The* (Cleveland) *Plain Dealer,* January 12, 1987.

"They were the greatest drives I've ever been involved with..." Tony Grossi, "Broncos End Browns' Dream, 23–20," *The* (Cleveland) *Plain Dealer,* January 12, 1987.

"That's the great thing about John..." Gene Williams, "Broncos Buck Long Odds as Elway Silences Critics," *The* (Cleveland) *Plain Dealer,* January 12, 1987.

"When you get a quarterback like Elway who can scramble..." Bob Dolgan, "Overtime Loss a Bitter Pill to Swallow for Browns," *The* (Cleveland) *Plain Dealer,* January 12, 1987.

"We definitely did not change our defense..." Chuck Heaton, "Browns Didn't Change Defense, Coach Says," *The* (Cleveland) *Plain Dealer,* January 12, 1987.

"When Rich Karlis got ready to kick the field goal..." Hanford Dixon, "I'm Sad, but We'll Be Back," Dawg Diary, *The* (Cleveland) *Plain Dealer,* January 12, 1987.

The Fumble

"There's a tremendous disappointment you are faced with..." Tony Grossi, "Broncos End Browns' Dream, 23–20," *The* (Cleveland) *Plain Dealer,* January 12, 1987.

"I told them I knew how disappointed they were..." Chuck Heaton, "Browns Didn't Change Defense, Coach Says," *The* (Cleveland) *Plain Dealer,* January 12, 1987.

"I broke to the outside and cut..." Tony Grossi, "Super Letdown," *The* (Cleveland) *Plain Dealer,* January 18, 1988.

"I thought I'd be looking at another 90-yard drive..." Paul Hoynes, "Steal, Smile from above Aid Broncos," *The* (Cleveland) *Plain Dealer,* January 18, 1988.

"Earnest is, without a doubt, one of the classiest..." Tony Grossi, "Byner Praised by Teammates," *The* (Cleveland) *Plain Dealer,* January 18, 1988.

"I told Earnest that this football team would not be..." Tony Grossi, "Super Letdown," *The* (Cleveland) *Plain Dealer*, January 18, 1988.

"I said I felt bad for him and that I knew that play..." Bill Livingston, "Kosar Brilliant, but Browns' Defense Fails Him," *The* (Cleveland) *Plain Dealer*, January 18, 1988.

"Words can't really describe the feelings..." Bill Livingston, "Kosar Brilliant, but Browns' Defense Fails Him," *The* (Cleveland) *Plain Dealer*, January 18, 1988.

"You don't get too many opportunities in life to get a second chance..." Gene Williams, "Newsome Is Feeling the Pain," *The* (Cleveland) *Plain Dealer*, January 18, 1988.

"It didn't hurt me as much as the Indianapolis game..." Tony Grossi, "Byner Praised by Teammates," *The* (Cleveland) *Plain Dealer*, January 18, 1988.

"I'm not in great spirits..." Tony Grossi, "Byner Praised by Teammates," *The* (Cleveland) *Plain Dealer*, January 18, 1988.

The King of Cleveland—Bernie Kosar

"Everything that could go wrong did go wrong..." Halberstam, David, *The Education of a Coach*, New York: Hyperion, 2005.

"Not to move your team to another city..." Halberstam, David, *The Education of a Coach*, New York: Hyperion, 2005.

A City Abandoned

"I had no choice..." Tom Feran and Roger Browns, "A Graceless Gov. Glendening Drops Browns Bomb at Infamous Gathering," *The* (Cleveland) *Plain Dealer*, November 7, 1995.

"I think our challenge..." Marla Ridenour, "Tagliabue Says NFL Needs Team in Cleveland," *The Columbus Dispatch*, December 11, 1995.

Memorable Games

"Cleveland is not going to take a black eye..." Bill Livingston, "Lerner, Policy Not Much above Fans," *The* (Cleveland) *Plain Dealer*, December 17, 2001.

"Everybody controlled themselves..." Bill Livingston, "Lerner, Policy Not Much above Fans," *The* (Cleveland) *Plain Dealer*, December 17, 2001.

"This is a victory..." Tony Grossi, "Browns Survive Jets Crash," *The* (Cleveland) *Plain Dealer*, January 4, 1987.

Memorable Figures

"He's full of charm and charisma..." Mary Kay Cabot, "Legend's on the Map," *The* (Cleveland) *Plain Dealer*, November 20, 2001.